S0-ARN-458

The Way We Were

The Way We Were

A Story of Conversion and Renewal

Joan Chittister

ORBIS BOOKS

Maryknoll, New York 10545

Founded in 1970, Orbis Books endeavors to publish works that enlighten the mind, nourish the spirit, and challenge the conscience. The publishing arm of the Maryknoll Fathers and Brothers, Orbis seeks to explore the global dimensions of the Christian faith and mission, to invite dialogue with diverse cultures and religious traditions, and to serve the cause of reconciliation and peace. The books published reflect the views of their authors and do not represent the official position of the Maryknoll Society. To learn about Maryknoll and Orbis Books, please visit our website at www.maryknoll.org.

Copyright © 2005 by Joan Chittister.

Published by Orbis Books, Maryknoll, NY 10545-0308.

All rights reserved.

No part of this publication may be reproduced or transmitted in any form or by any means, electronic or mechanical, including photocopying, recording, or any information storage or retrieval system, without prior permission in writing from the publisher.

Queries regarding rights and permissions should be addressed to: Orbis Books, P.O. Box 308, Maryknoll, NY 10545-0308.

Manufactured in the United States of America.

Library of Congress Cataloging-in-Publication Data

Chittister, Joan.
    The way we were : a story of conversion and renewal / by Joan Chittister.
      p. cm.
    ISBN 1-57075-577-9 (pbk.)
    1. Benedictine Sisters of Erie – History – 20th century. I. Title.
BX4278.E6C45 2005
271'.97 – dc22

                       2005004291

Contents

Introduction

NOT TOO LONG AGO, it took five days to send a letter;
people went to school, worked, bought a house, and died
in the same towns in which they had been born; eating meat on
Friday was a mortal sin; Catholics and Protestants didn't inter-
marry; there were no women in Congress; almost no one you
knew traveled outside the country; and God was unquestion-
ably an avuncular male. The universe was a huge Newtonian
clock, life was what we could see by looking at it, and truth
was both discernible and immutable.

Then, all of a sudden, even grandmothers were using computers and sending e-mail to friends; men and women left
small towns for large cities and big jobs and high-rise condos
and retirement villages; women got PhD's; Catholics married
Hindus as well as Protestants; a woman ran for vice president of the United States; students began to go to Rome on
class trips as easily as they had once gone to amusement
parks down the road; someone invented a bomb that threatened to annihilate the globe; Newton's clock was found not to
be as orderly as we had thought; and God became pure Spirit
again.

Education, politics, government, science, marriage, and even
religion changed dramatically in the twentieth century. We
learned exciting new things about the nature of life.

We found ourselves, telescopes in hand, space stations in
place, looking at a whole different structure of the universe
than we had been long taught to expect. At the beginning of
the century, we taught that there was one galaxy, and we were
it. By the end of the century, we taught that there were millions
of galaxies and we were one of the smallest.

It was an entire century of New Beginnings; it was a century when we began to begin to think differently about almost everything we had ever learned.

It was no time for business as usual. Every institution on earth had begun to change.

The change affected our very psyches. We no longer thought about things the way the generation before us had. We learned that there was no such thing as "authority." No one had all the answers anymore. There were only "authorities," only a series of experts on whose interpretations the meaning of life seemed to depend but who all differed even among themselves.

Life was not a pyramid, we came to understand. Life was a weave of differences in concert. But the psyche reeled at the loss of old compass points and the uncertainty of new ones. Alvin Toffler in his seminal work, *Future Shock*, had been warning the world for decades about the possibility that the human mind would not be able to absorb the rapidity of change as quickly as technology would be able to communicate it. And the tensions underlying every transformation that each change brought only served to prove his point.

At the same time, the shifting of the tectonic plates of society, under what had seemed to us to be timeless institutions, affected our souls as well. Change certainly impacted the way we thought about religion and the way religions thought about us, about the ways of a creating God with the nature that had been created. It led us all to wonder again about who we were really meant to be, how we were really meant to function, what we were really about on this earth.

In society we called it the New Science, meaning evolution, quantum physics, molecular biology, and chaos theory. In the church, we called it Vatican II. These two streams of being, science and religion, the two pillars of life — one ancient and, at least apparently, unchanging, the other kinetic and unpredictable — crossed paths in ways that changed both our concepts of life and our understandings of spiritual growth.

Social scientists called the phenomenon a "paradigm shift," a way of seeing the world differently than we had ever seen it before. The church of Vatican II called it "renewal."

This book is about what happened to one group in particular and to all of us in general at the crossroads of these two great changes in worldview. It deals with questions of how change comes about and how leadership affects the process and the progress of it. But it also looks at what happens to the people who are caught in the abyss of it and what those experiences have to say to the rest of us about the future of once flourishing institutions at a time of cataclysmic change. Finally, it tells us something about the spiritual upheaval and insights that underlie and drive the current change.

In order to put flesh on the bones of theory, this book on the spiritual dimensions of global change is written through the experiences and eyes of one group of women religious, the Benedictine Sisters of Erie, who celebrate the 150th anniversary of their community in 2006. Whether there will ever be the 250th anniversary of this group depends, of course, on the vagaries of society and the resilience of the members. No group is completely in charge of its own social destiny. Things happen to us all that are out of our control. But for us as one group, in an order that traces its roots back over fifteen hundred years, successful transition from one worldview to another surely depends on the spiritual choices we pursue in the face of the course of history around us.

In this case, the evolution of the community depended as much on conversion of heart as it did on the ordinary processes of social change, though the nature of social change was itself the current that carried the process to fulfillment. Underneath it all, however, basic to its completion was the nature of conversion itself. The real questions were not institutional ones; the real questions were spiritual ones. They involved the very meaning of the life of the group as well as the commitment level of its individual members. The questions the group faced were not only organizational: Does renewal depend on change or adaptation? Does it require continuity or disconti-nuity? What is it that makes a group receptive to change and when is change more harmful to a group than life-giving. As endemic to the process as these questions always are at mo-ments of great social upheaval, the questions that affected the group most deeply, that caused the deepest ruptures of soul, that threatened the very cohesion of the group were spiritual: Would change destroy the original impetus and meaning of what we have always known as "religious" life?

Or to put it more concretely: What led women religious, those stable models of perpetual regularity, to rewrite their age-old rules, to recast the most public details of their private lives? What did it mean for the meaning of religious life? What did it cost them as individuals, as groups? And, finally, where did it lead them and what is it saying about the place of change in the spiritual as well as the social lives of us all? Those questions de-manded "conversion of life," as the Benedictine tradition puts it in the vow ceremony that binds a monastic's future to a Benedictine lifestyle.

To understand the degree of change demanded in this period it helps to understand the issues in question. The pillars of the institutional world rest on two things: on ideas and on struc-tures. Garden variety change usually involves a transmutation in one or the other. When ideas change but structures remain stable, it is simply a matter of learning a new reason for doing an established task. When structures change but ideas remain stable, it is normally simply a matter of learning a new way to perform an established task. But when both structures and ideas change at the same time, the result is a crossover point in the history of the enterprise. And that is exactly what happened in the period about which this book is written.

Then change becomes the very essence, the very zenith of existence. Change itself becomes the nucleus of life. Then the ability to negotiate change may well measure the difference be-tween social effectiveness and social decline, between longevity and untimely dissolution, between social impact and social irrelevance.

One thing is for sure: change becomes the elixir of life, guaranteeing wholeness, pointing toward liberation, threatening dissolution. But change is not for its own sake. It promises newness but requires a love for the past if the new present that it ushers in is to have enough meaning and momentum to carry it beyond the mere seductions of novelty.

The central focus of this book is the period from 1965 to 1990, or what is now euphemistically called "the renewal period of religious life." It covers three different administrations in our community and three very different leadership styles and tasks. It changed the lifestyle, works, and developmental processes of its members. It cost all of them their entire lives.

Religious life itself became the centrifuge of spiritual conversion, the very stuff of faith, the sea of change in which the Will of God — once clearly cast in age-old structures — now rocked and turned, gyrated and changed almost from day to day.

This thing called "renewal" changed their very way of being in the world. But in the end, it may not have really changed anything at all. Maybe the only thing that really changed is the way they went on being what they had always intended to be in the first place.

The question is, What does that have to say to the rest of us in the course of our own lives and ongoing challenges to be true to who we say we are and faithful to what we say we do?

To navigate real change, we're told, demands both deep roots and strong wings. This book is about what it demanded of one group to maintain a balance and survive the tension between the two. This book is about surviving change, the cataclysm of perpetual irregularity.

As a young sister I watched Mother Sylvester, my first prioress, carefully. How did it feel, I wondered after a year or two in the monastery, to get up every morning knowing that there was no one around who could tell you what to do all day. The rest of us, after all, were herded through every minute. Minutely defined schedules controlled every minute of every day. The Customs Book prescribed every behavior. There were few exceptions, few alterations, almost never a change. The prioress alone, it seemed, was free to do as she pleased. Then I grew up and became prioress and discovered that no one person in particular tells a prioress what to do: they all do. In fact, orchestrating the demands of a group, shaping the nature of a group to the demands of the world around it is of the essence of leadership.

The period of religious life from 1965 to 1990 tested all the theories of leadership and change ever developed. It did not feel like "renewal" then. It felt like disaster, like loss, like liberation, like life gone wild. And it felt like all of them all at once. Most of all, it felt rudderless and out of control. Finding the way through a period for which there was no recent model, no rule book, no spiritual guide colored the years with both a giddy joy and a fearsome shadow. How would we know that what we were doing was right? How would we know how far to go? Who would decide?

Leadership, after all, is key to change. The right to determine the agenda of a group is the ultimate power in any organizational deliberations. Leadership determines what questions will be asked by a group and how far the group is permitted to go in answering them. That takes organizational leadership skill, of course. At the end of the day, however, the personalities and spiritual vision of the leaders of the Erie community of that period, as well as their leadership strategies, organizational skills, or history of the period, made all the difference in the pace and direction of change, at least for the Benedictine Sisters of Erie.

The leadership of the Erie Benedictines during this refounding period rested in three women, each of them very different in background, personality, and vision, each of them very focused on different aspects of community life. But together they embodied the three faces of change that mark the movement of an institution from one era of history to another. Alice Schierberl began the deconstruction of pre–Vatican II religious life. Mary Margaret Kraus enabled the development of new directions and the testing of new values. I myself set out in the midst of the disintegration of past models of life and ministry to launch a process of revitalization. The task now was to enable the group to find its way into new directions without losing the core values of the past, to become a new kind of presence in the world without abandoning the meaning and bedrock of what had been the very essence of the life for centuries.

It was not an easy undertaking or a simple venture. It may even be seen by history as having been an impossible one. But the choices were clear. There were too many things changing around us to think for a moment that we could simply stand still in the midst of it and will it all to go away, to pass us by, to leave us untouched. The only possible direction lay ahead of us. The options were uncompromising: change or die, begin again or simply live out the rest of life like leaves on a tree in winter time. The tradition we carried in our hearts brought with it almost fifteen hundred years of successful transition from one period of history to another. This was no time to give up without trying.

But how?

Sometime between 1960 and 1990 the Benedictine Sisters of Erie, as the city had known them for over a hundred years, disappeared and then, just as suddenly, reemerged in ways the city never expected. Situated on Erie's lower east side, once the hub of a port town, now its "inner city," half-hidden from sight — semicloistered, uniformed, entrenched in seven grade schools and four high schools within a hundred miles of the monastery — they resurfaced somehow in vibrant new local projects and in global associations on the national stage everywhere. In thirty short years, after a lifetime of doing nothing but classroom teaching, they had opened soup kitchens, worked in chanceries and ecological projects, developed educational programs for welfare students, gone to foreign missions, opened halfway houses, retreat centers, housing sites for the elderly, and even wound up in jail for protesting the Vietnam War.

By 1990 most of the schools were gone, habits were a thing of the past, cloister was an anachronism. How such a transformation of a long-established lifestyle could happen within thirty years to an entire group whose cultural history extends back fifteen centuries is a question of no small import. Whole university departments devote themselves to the study of change. This book purports to trace it in one particular situation, not so much chronologically — a project already documented in Sister Stephanie Campbell's *Visions of Change, Voices of Challenge*[1] — as it does emotionally and theologically.

The social psychology of change is real theory but change is what happens to real people. The questions that surround it are as personal as they are theoretical. Why after all these years would change of such magnitude happen? What were the struggles, the obstacles, the experiences of change? For what gains and at what cost was change accomplished? And, finally, as a result, what has happened to the quality and character of a life the origin of which stretches back in largely uninterrupted development to the sixth century?

What has happened in one place to one people in our own times can, perhaps, give both light and hope to individuals and groups everywhere in whose own lives change seems to be more cataclysm than gift.

Change has three faces: deconstruction, development, and revitalization. None of them is easy. Each of them is exciting. Most important of all, all of them, if we allow them to be, are life-giving.

e. e. cummings wrote once, "All creation begins with destruction." We know.

Part One

The Way We Were

1

Icons of Changelessness

"C HANGE AMUSES THE MIND, yet scarcely profits," Goethe wrote in the eighteenth century. The dictum had the ring of wisdom, and if not wisdom, certainly of monastic custom. Built on a rule of life written in the sixth century when the rhythm of human development followed the agricultural cycle and days were evenly balanced to match it, calm and constancy were the order of the day.

When Mother Sylvester Groner left office in 1958 after eight years as formation director and twelve years as prioress, she turned over to her successor, Mother Alice Schierberl, a community whose life had been built on regularity, uniformity, and continuity. She herself had been a quiet woman, stable and soft-spoken. She had quiet eyes and an infectious smile. I never heard her tell a joke, but she laughed easily at stories told by others, loved to watch a community party, and spoke straight, clear talk.

At the interview I had with her as part of the established pre-entrance process, she marked out the subjects I would be taking to complete my high school education: history, English, chemistry, physics, and French. "But, Mother," I said, "I don't like French." She looked up over her glasses at me as, I learned later, she was wont to do at what she considered moments of horror. "My dear child," she said, "we don't say we don't like *anything*." I thought a minute. "Do we lie?" I said back. I can still see her bite her upper lip to stop the smile and look away.

But, weeks later, when my schedule came out, I found myself, nevertheless, assigned to a Spanish class.

Mother Sylvester was a steady personality, given neither to displays of deep gloom nor to outbursts of delirious highs. She steered a steady ship. And the effects of it showed in the lifestyle of the community.

Life under Mother Sylvester was marked by the rigors of routine. Every morning her office door opened after breakfast by 7:30 a.m., and the small light on her desk glowed late into the night, day after day after day. Her phone number, professed members liked to recall, was 53012. "Her working hours," the older sisters said. "From 5:30 a.m. to midnight." Her pattern varied seldom, if at all, and the community's standards shadowed hers. The group operated on norms of hard work and discipline, of faithfulness to routine and commitment to self-control. It was a good life. Predictable to the point of being dull, perhaps, but good. Difficult in its persistent commitment to implacable rules and repetition, but good. Change was anathema; repetition, regularity, and "fidelity" to the Rule constituted real holiness.

The most important quality of all about the life at that time, perhaps, is that there were few, if any, questions about the nature of it. And why would there be? The church valorized and encouraged religious life at every level of education, tradition had enshrined it, and the public supported it. Catholic parents prayed that at least one of their children would enter religious life. To have a religious in the family stood for many, in fact, as the hallmark of the good Catholic home.

Up until the period of the two world wars when women began to be needed in society to substitute for men in the armed forces, the difference between the lives of women in convents and the lives of women in the home was far less distinct than might be assumed. Women in religious life did not often leave the premises and never unaccompanied. Neither did laywomen in medieval Europe or Victorian England or rural America. Independence of movement marked women of the lower class, perhaps, but not "nice" women.

Women in religious life were concentrated on domestic duties and pious practices or the education of children. So were women in the secular world. Women everywhere spent their lives cleaning and praying and child-rearing. Those things were "women's work," "God's will for them."

Women in convents had no personal monies, little independence, and, at the highest levels of ecclesiastical jurisprudence, lived at the mercy of male superiors. So did women in the home. The church, the courts, and the family all gave men control of a woman's property, her intellectual development, her personal behavior, and her public participation. Women were the "weaker sex," the "helpmates" of creation, the adult children of male overseers. If anything, life in a convent gave options for female intellectual development that few laywomen enjoyed except for those who could go away to study in order to become "good wives and mothers." In monasteries, at least, history, literature, and science could be studied for their own sake, for professional development rather than for social accomplishment.

Dedicated to spiritual development and intent on public service, convent life for women honed all the social assumptions about women to a fine point. Religious life in the Erie Benedictines in the late 1950s, as it had been for years, was marked by five basic characteristics: it was reflective, regular, focused, clear, and effective.

Reflection, an essential part of Benedictine monasticism, formed the skeletal structure of the life. Everything else in a sister's life was scheduled around it. Choral prayer, the public prayer of the entire community, went on seven times a day.

The community rose at 5:30 a.m. to pray Lauds, Prime, and Terce — three of the seven traditional "Hours" of the Divine Office — do thirty minutes of "spiritual reading," and attend Mass, all before breakfast in the morning.

None, or noon prayer, was prayed by those sisters who remained in the monastery during the day while the others taught in parochial school classrooms in the area.

Matins, the office of readings, and Vespers, what should have been evening prayer, were recited at 4:45 p.m., a prayer period easily sixty to ninety minutes long, depending on the nature of the feast day.

Compline or night prayer signaled the end of the active day at 7:30 p.m. every evening.

All in all, the community prayed together, on average, almost four hours a day, every day of the week.

It was a life immersed in ideas, psalms, scripture readings, and the spiritual writings of the ages. Pieces of psalms, scraps of parables, mantras of antiphons, passages from Augustine, Basil, the Gregories, Bernard of Clairveaux, the whole panoply of early Christian writers, punctuated every segment of life. It was a life of silence, of quiet, of thought. But, don't be fooled, it was not a life of holy leisure. Outside of prayer, the Bene-dictine sister went nonstop for the other twelve hours of the waking day. She spent a minimum of nine of those hours in classroom activities. The remaining three hours she spent at meals, household tasks, and class preparation.

Regularity, the hidebound commitment to making tomor-row exactly the same as yesterday, marked the entire life. Life outside the round of prayers was as regular as life inside the chapel. Everyone had a schedule. Everyone lived within it. There was a set time for everything: a time to do the daily sweeping and the weekend cleaning, a time to wait on tables, a time to clean halls and do chapel linens and wash windows and dust high ledges or polish low ledges and bake altar breads and make coifs and be on phone duty and serve the priest's breakfast and wash down the stairs or sweep out the garden moat and buff the tiled halls.

And in between it all, a sister taught and prepared lesson plans and corrected papers and took college courses herself to make up for the uninterrupted college education she was unlikely to get in a period of the burgeoning Catholic school system and the voracious need for nun-teachers. Instead, women religious took evening classes and weekend courses and went to summer school while they taught and did everything else as well. It was a schedule that repeated itself season after season and year after year every year of their lives.

The regularity itself became part of the spiritual quality of the life. There were no distractions, no foolish waste of time, no fragmentation. The routine, the repetitious, and the habitual, with all those implied for an unceasing promise of security, became part of the religious discipline — confused with it, substituted for it, required by it. After all, if nothing changed there was nothing to fear. Life simply went on, basically unaltered, surely unalterable. "Commitment" some people called it.

The strength of the life lay in its unyielding clarity of *focus*, both spiritual and professional. No one asked what a sister did because everyone already knew. They prayed, they taught, and they lived lives of ascetic invariability together.

The answer brooked little, if any, quarrel. After all, what else could a sister do? She lived to love God and to serve others, both of which commitments had already been decided and scheduled for her years before by people much wiser than she in the ways of the Spirit. It was a life of renunciation, penance, and prayer. What else was there in the spiritual life?

In the end, it was precisely the theological *clarity* of the life that accounted for both its attraction and for the seeds of aversion to religious life as well. "You can't go to the convent," my uncles told me. "We love the sisters but you weren't made to be a sister," they went on. "With your personality, you'll be bored to death."

But the life promised "the hundredfold," that promise of heavenly reward and recompense for whatever its losses in family, friends, fortune, and fun. This was the "higher vocation." This was what people did who really loved God. The other world, the next world, made the sacrifices of this world not just doable but desirable.

Finally, religious life of the 1950s was *effective*. Large groups of women, assigned to a common task and working without financial recompense, simply gave their professional lives to the task of educating a Catholic population for success in a white, Anglo-Saxon world. They had no family life to make demands on their attention, no expectations of personal space or time, few or no professional expenses, no prescribed wardrobes, and no private space to furnish or maintain. On the backs of this nameless, faceless, labor force rose the largest private social service system in the United States, and it was free, or nearly so, to all who used it.

Who could doubt the value of such a life to the church, to the people, to the country? Who could argue that doing such a thing was not a noble task? Reflective, stable, focused, clear, and effective, religious life was a magnet for young women who sought to live a life that, at the same time, offered both noble purpose and spiritual reward. It was not without cost, of course, but until now at least, the cost was little calculated and ever more confirmed.

2

The Waxing and Waning of Passion

T HE MONK GIVING the retreat that year was clear and to the
point: "The thing that worries me about nuns," he said as
he looked out over the quiet chapel, all backs up straight, all
hands hidden under their scapulars, "is that they are like swans
on water: they look so placid as they go floating across a pond
but underneath they are kicking furiously." I was sitting in the
chapel. I knew he was right. I just didn't know yet that the
struggle might be more a sign of sanity than it was of sanctity.
It was hard to tell which impulse had gained the ascendancy:
the struggle to maintain the self or the struggle to repress the
self. It became even harder to know which grappling was really
of the essence of holiness.

The ideal, of course, was passionless acceptance of a kind
of perverse suppression of the self. "Offering it up," and "accepting the will of God" were the mantras of holiness. The
reality was that the struggles were indicators of questions that
needed desperately to be asked: Was suppression of the self
really meant to be offered up? Was acceptance of an organizational will for the will of God an adequate substitute for free
will and personal responsibility? Was a life without passion
truly a holy life?

Life as we lived it in the 1950s worked. At least at one level.
It was sincerely reflective, unalterably regular, totally focused,
unsparingly clear, and professionally effective to a fault. But
there was another level of it, not as publicly apparent but just as

internally real. It was just as likely, depending on the day, to feel boringly reflective, distressingly regular, inhumanely focused, tediously clear, and gruelingly effective, as well.

By the mid-twentieth century, religious life, as well as being centered in God and totally engaged in the great missionary endeavors of the eighteenth and nineteenth centuries, had settled down into a kind of life that was now rigid, isolated, dependent, overworked, and fast becoming spiritually trivialized, as opposed to spiritually significant. The passion of its early pioneers, for whom the establishment of foundations and the development of educational systems had once been the stuff of vision and dreams, had given way to the kind of professional satisfaction that comes with success.

What religious of the nineteenth century had set out to do had been largely accomplished:

First, the faith had been preserved in all its many forms and shapes. In one small town in the Diocese of Erie, four different ethnic churches faced one another on opposite corners of the street — the Polish parish church, the Slavic parish church, the German parish church, and the Italian parish church. And all of them had their own grade school attached, each of which taught classes in the language of their tradition as well as in English.

Catholicism in the United States was not only universal; it was, at the same time, very, very particular, very, very ethnic. And so, it seems, was religious life. Assimilation was clearly not the issue in the Catholic community, whatever the myth of the national melting pot. Every nationality, it seemed, had its own sisters who worked with their own people: the Polish Nazarenes, the Irish Mercys, the French Josephs, and the German Benedictines. The Erie Benedictines were founded from Germany, for instance, and to this day sing German hymns at Christmas time.

Second, the country's Catholic minority had been integrated into a largely Protestant society. The names of Catholic war dead enshrined in Catholic church foyers everywhere earned the right for the entire population to finally be considered trustworthy citizens of the United States. In Oil City, Pennsylvania, as recently as the 1960s, no Catholic had ever taught in its public schools, but Catholic students were there in growing numbers, the real sign of things to come. At the same time, Catholic hospitals were now beginning to receive federal funding and Catholic candidates were beginning to run for public office. John F. Kennedy's accession to the presidency of the country signaled the end of the Catholic ghetto once and for all and with it the perennial accusations of papists as more citizens of Rome than citizens of the country.

Thirdly, a Catholic professional class, educated and articulate, was now on the threshold of civil society. The Catholic school system, long undersubsidized and underequipped, had nevertheless managed to produce generation after generation of students who were now graduating from college, going into corporate America, rising to positions of academic and professional prominence. The Catholic voice was beginning to emerge everywhere, timidly at first, perhaps, but more and more sure of itself, more and more "American" all the time.

If the notion that Catholicism had finally come of age in the United States was really the case, so was the notion that whatever had brought us to this point had to be continued, intact and entire, bigger and better. Everywhere, class size got larger, nuns were more in demand, the work load increased.

"Performance punishes," a friend of mine says. What she knows from her own experience the academicians confirm from one period of history to another. The organizational life cycle, theorists maintain, has various clear and recognizable stages. In the first stage of organizational development, a dream bursts into being: to rescue children from the streets, to teach girls as well as boys to read, to comfort the dying, to defend the faith. At this stage of development, no effort is too much or, more to the point, no effort feels like effort at all, so intense is the vision, so immediate the need.

Eventually, however, these early periods of charismatic energy turn to the level of deadening standardization. Then life

settles into the routine of repeating what works and the institution expands to its farthermost edge, to the point where it
will not only never get bigger but will even begin to see signs
of decline.

When routine replaces vision, when the organization ex-
hausts its internal possibilities and hones its services to a fine
point, when the mountain of challenge that brought it into
being has been scaled, when new needs emerge in the society
that this particular institution either cannot or will not ad-
dress, its social impact declines and its effectiveness with it.
As Catholics integrated more and more into society at large,
moved into the suburbs, and sent their own children to larger,
better equipped, and, at the same time, less expensive schools,
Catholic education as the Catholic bulwark against a hostile
world began to wane. Catholics no longer sought refuge from
the world around them, in the first place, and, in the second place, were no longer even sure bulwarks were desirable.
They sought to be like the people around them, not part of an
identifiably suspicious subculture. Catholicism was no longer
a system under siege.

When I first began to teach in the parochial schools that
our community had staffed for years, sisters were still being
spat on in the streets of the small towns where Catholics were
a minority. By the time I left those places ten years later, the
Catholic schools sat half empty. Catholic parents had begun to
shift their children to the larger central system with its winning
football teams and well-equipped band programs and broader
academic offerings. And they were accepted without regard for
religion. Whether we knew it then or not the role of nuns would
change with the changing social patterns that had brought us
to this point.

Religious life ironically, after decades of pioneering vitality, was by this time in the process of standardizing with a
vengeance. The effect of that routinization on the character of
religious life itself can never be overestimated.

Rigidity descended on what had been the community's creative beginnings. Young nuns from Germany had moved into

small family houses in the middle of American cities, learned the new language, lived with the pupils they taught, mixed and moved with the people freely, and took upon themselves whole new ways living. Within twenty-five years of coming to Erie, they had expanded the community to send small groups of sisters — two or three at a time — to outlying areas over sixty miles away. The monastery became the whole monastic community wherever it was, however it lived, not simply those who lived in the motherhouse in Erie. There were no obsessions with cloister here. No distancing themselves here, as they had done in Europe, from the world around them.

By the 1950s those days of endless creativity, of ready response to new needs, had quietly disappeared. Somewhere along the line, someone had produced for the community a precisely written Customs Book, itself a contradiction in terms since laws, not customs, are the things meant to be written down. Customs, in the truest sense of the word, live in the heart of a group and so change with a change in group experience or feelings.

Customs are the things we always do because they give particular dimensions of life certain levels of emotional meaning — like decorate Christmas trees with family pictures, or bake birthday cakes, or color Easter eggs together. No, the community "customs" book was not meant to add meaning to life. It was meant to control life down to its finest points. This Customs Book prescribed for the minutiae of life.

The Customs Book contained rules against "talking on the street" or "going out alone" or "visiting in parlors" or even "eating between meals" or "sitting on the side of her bed." A sister's life had begun to be described in minute detail. Living a good religious life came to mean that there were precise ways to hold a breviary, precise postures to use when bowing during prayer, precise times to go to bed, precise times to speak and not to speak, even to another sister. We learned how to break the bread we put on our dinner plates to remind us of the "five wounds of Jesus," and how to bow to statues and sisters in the halls and what words to say to ask for permissions, as in "Mother, for the love of Jesus, may I..." or "Um Jesus willem...." "Custom," social psychologists point out, begins, in any society, to take on the form of law. In this one, custom ran the risk of becoming morality, as well.

The difference between religious society and most other social situations is that in an open society custom evolves within the bowels of a group, out of the needs of the members. In the religious life of the 1950s, authority — somebody's authority somewhere — began to be the source of "custom," and no one ever asked the members whether what was being required was really meeting their needs at all. The point became simply to keep the customs, not to evaluate them.

The social isolation that emerged out of such rigidity had major implications for the role and public impact of a religious life that was meant to serve the people. For obvious historical reasons, cloister, in the strict sense of the word, had never existed for American Benedictine women to the extent it had for nuns in Europe. In its place, however, there developed a cloister mentality meant to blend the two cultural situations that was more confusing than the thought of cloister itself.

We did not exist entirely behind walls. We went wherever our work demanded. We left the monastery daily to teach school. We shopped when necessary. We went out to conferences and liturgies and public events.

Pupils and parents came in as well, either to visit the sisters or to work with them. But the sisters seldom, if ever, went out to visit or work with the people. Unless, of course, they had special permission to do so, which, outside of emergency situations, was rarely given.

For a sister to appear at a hospital bedside of a sick relative was a sure sign that the person was dying. I remember quite clearly my own uncle making me promise not to come if he ever got sick, just in case my presence there might tip his luck or, worse, cause the heart attack he was trying to avoid.

Sisters did not simply "drop in" at home to see their elderly parents. The parents were expected to come to the monastery if they wanted to see their daughters — however difficult a trip that might be for them — or else never see them at all. Sisters did not take bread to the homes of the elderly, whatever their needs. The community chapel and periods of choral prayer were not open to laypeople, even on Christmas Eve. It was a life within a life, a subculture defined outside the mainstream by its own property, its own clothing, its own lifestyle, and its own customs. It was insulated, isolated, and limiting.

Equally as difficult, either to explain to new members or to understand on the personal level as the years went by, was the degree of dependence that such rigidity and isolation implied. Full-grown adult women, women with advanced degrees from the best universities in the country, made few, if any, personal decisions. They could administer schools and hospitals, get professional education, build buildings, and manage finances but they couldn't decide for themselves whether to work in school on a Saturday or not. They "spoke fault" every month for "spilling food and water, losing pins, wasting soap, spotting a scapular." They could not drive cars. They had no money, even for the most personal of needs. "By accident, I was left in a school building alone in 1964," Sister Mary Regina recalls, "with no way to get home and no way to make a phone call for help. So I wrote a letter to the superior in Erie about it. Finally, a letter came back later saying that sisters should be given dimes to carry with them when they went out." And this in an era when women everywhere were beginning to take personal decision-making for granted, when teenage girls held paying jobs and the bank accounts that went with them, when women were beginning to talk about choosing a career as well as finding a husband.

The intellectual schizophrenia such a situation engendered began to show. New members started to ask "why" we did what we did. It soon became clear that, unlike the generation before them, they did not find the answers persuasive. If they got any answers at all. In the place of answers came the spiritualization of trivia.

Benedictine monasticism, traditionally based in the strong scriptural foundation of the Liturgy of the Hours became, for women at least, encrusted, almost obscured, by "practices" of private piety and a very limited theology of an obedience that was more military than discerning. From that perspective, the stuff of high sanctity came to be rendered in terms of childlike docility to otherwise mindless matters such as not swinging their arms while they walked or praying with outstretched arms after Compline. As a result, the simple life became simplistic. Whether this was done to women to make up for their lack of theological education or done by women to make their otherwise uneducated lives meaningful, who can say? The point is only that, in a church that denied theology degrees to women until the mid-1960s, their spiritual lives failed to keep pace with their professional educations.

The sisters "spoke fault" on their knees regularly to develop humility. The idea was a good one, perhaps, an attempt more than likely to make real the chapter in the Rule of Benedict "On Humility." The fourth degree of humility, Benedict taught in the sixth century, was that a monastic "hide from the abbot none of the evil thoughts in his heart but take them and dash them on the rock that was Christ." This call to unmask the ego, to trust the spiritual lights of another, to open ourselves to guidance is a healthy one. Speaking fault as it had come down to us was not.

When every minor behavior of life — spilling food or losing pins — begins to have the same moral value as life's major ones, one of two things is likely to happen: either nothing continues to have much real moral value at all or everything has equal value and all of life becomes a moral torment. Spiritual directors called it "scrupulosity," priests called it "pin-stealing." Psychologists called it "neurosis" or "underdevelopment." Early generations internalized the moral leveling. Little by little, later generations, postwar vocations, did not.

For those who valued the life at its best — its reflectiveness, regularity, focus, clarity, and effectiveness — the only way to negotiate the cognitive dissonance of its dark side was to begin to ignore the forms of it in favor of the faith it reflected. The oral history of the community is replete with stories of community heroes over the years who simply disregarded and transcended the norms.

Sister Marie Claire owned a record player and played it every Sunday afternoon despite the fact that individual sisters were not permitted to own record players. Marie Claire was a music teacher and said she needed it for her work. Which is no doubt true at one level. But she needed it for her mental health, too, and she said so.

Sisters Rose and Pauline went home to see their elderly parents when none of the rest of the community ever even thought of walking into a normal home. The need was obvious, they said, and so they did it.

Sister Patricia coached the girls' basketball team and traveled with them to every game. As local superior, Sister Bernadette gave the community regular parties to take the pressure off the endless grind of duties.

Sister Mary Ann made cookies and left them out in the kitchen on large cookie sheets to be taken at will even when eating between meals was forbidden.

Sister Rosemary never missed a trip, called all of them "education," and said she considered it imperative that the sisters "keep up with the times."

Sister Lois Marie went into the homes of families and students years before it was either a practice or a virtue.

Sister Theophane worked long into the night, when the house was its most quiet, despite the fact that the curfew was 10:00 p.m. Most important of all, however, is the obvious: all of these things were totally innocent behaviors made opprobrious by rules that should never have been written, let alone obeyed.

Clearly, the human spirit does not die easily. Those who kept it alive in the community kept the community itself healthy enough to be capable of survival. For those who had internalized the substitution of behaviors for the development of depth of soul and greatness of spirit, the way back to fullness of life was difficult indeed.

In an atmosphere of rigidity, isolation, dependence, and the spiritualization of the mundane, work became the center of the life, and the schedule became the altar on which the sacrifice of life was made. Sisters prayed, worked, prayed again, worked, prayed, ate, and "recreated," meaning talked to one another for forty-five minutes after supper, prayed again, and did school work or household tasks till 10:00 p.m. Every day. All days. With little or no possibility of diversion from that schedule for their entire lives.

When Mother Sylvester Groner left office, she was sixty-five years old. Mother Alice Schierberl, who followed her, took office at the age of thirty-eight, a completely different generation of woman. She came from a position as high school principal. She knew young women and the world from which they came. She knew, too, the world into which they were coming and she valued it. But it was already on the verge of becoming more different than ever from the world in which these new candidates for the life had been formed.

3

Crosscurrents in Culture

H OWEVER STABLE AND IMMUTABLE religious life may have looked to distant observers when Alice Schierberl became prioress of the Benedictine Sisters of Erie in 1958, the architectural plates of society, those great pillars of social certainty on which the world had rested for centuries, were already beginning to shift in the world around us. The United States, recently relieved of the burden of three major wars in less than forty years, was poised to begin a whole new chapter of its development. The implications of those wars for the status, structures, economics, and expectations of U.S. society were only beginning to be apparent.

Society as we had always known it, with the norms and values developed in an earlier age, began to take on new shapes, think new thoughts. A paradigm shift, the assumptions on which we had built our personal as well as our public worlds, was in the making. The problem was that few people realized either what was happening or what was at stake.

A paradigm shift occurs in a society when the way we once thought about the world changes. When old truths — women are not fit for public life, for instance, or only Catholics go to heaven, or matter and spirit are two different things — no longer satisfy present questions or account for present circumstances, the foundation on which we base our assumptions about life begin to give way. If women really are humanly fit for public life — intellectually fit to think, psychologically fit to lead, fit to manage both emotionally and physically — then the notion of restricting the actions of women is groundless. If heaven is not a place in the sky, then the theology of Mary's Assumption into heaven must be recast. If matter and spirit are composed of the same molecules, one simply more densely packed than the other, then a religious definition of matter as worthless and spirit as better is at very least unworthy of a good theology of creation. Then a whole new way of living and thinking and evaluating life begins.

The point is that religious life did not change in a vacuum. Things were happening in the society around us that were approaching critical mass. New ideas were erupting everywhere that simply could not be stemmed. Industries long dormant or focused on the war effort were rolling consumer goods off the assembly lines in record time. Jobs were plentiful. Wages of the working class rose to astonishing new levels overnight. We had the atom bomb and all the security we thought it implied. The GI Bill provided a college education to thousands of returning soldiers. Women had stepped onto the public stage with jobs and educations of their own. It was an era pregnant with possibility. On the outside, everything looked normal. Sitcoms on the new TV still worked off the *Father Knows Best* model while, at the same time, *American Bandstand* signaled a coming age of new freedoms and new interests. Under the walls of old norms that had once formed the boundaries of our stable, predictable worlds, the termites were at work.

A paradigm shift greater than anything of its kind since Galileo — accelerated by a world at war, stretched by other cultures, and becoming every day more technological than mechanical — began little by little to alter even the givens of religious life. "This system, Sisters," Sister Mary Regina Flanagan, mathematics teacher, explained as she introduced the community to the complexities of the new binary number system on which the world's first computer had been built, "will change the world — change the way we live, change the way we do business, change the way we think." Little did we know.

The young woman who entered religious life in the late 1950s, therefore, found herself caught between her formation in the values of her parents' generation and the emerging expectations of her own. The erosion of those values that had given unqualified support to the very notion of religious life itself had already begun. Developments in the life sciences, theories of human sexuality, the changing role of women in society, and the emergence of globalism with its awareness that there are unlimited other ways to be holy, to be human, struck quietly but deeply at the traditional theological foundations of religious life. The assault came silently but not without impact.

Ironically, it was war — man's ultimate warrior occupation — that struck the deepest blow at the age-old definition of woman's role in society. Faced with the largest war effort in the history of the country and a Europe that had been largely decimated by the time the United States entered World War II, the mustering of major numbers of troops was large and long. First high school and college classes were emptied, then offices, then hospitals, then shops and industrial operations. Everywhere, including in the armed forces themselves, women were called upon to take the place of men now called into active duty in campaigns on foreign soil.

"Rosie the Riveter," the government poster of the woman patriot on the assembly lines that kept American industry operating in wartime, became the classic icon of the new woman: strong, capable, and as important to the social order outside the home as she was within it. Not only did the image of woman change in society, it changed within women themselves. Woman as debutante, wallflower, clinging vine, or china doll faded from view. And the whole idea that once the war was over women would simply quietly retire to home and hearth went with them. Women had discovered a new sense of their own abilities and significance. Going back quietly to the cloister of the kitchen had lost its appeal. Women had suddenly found other roles to play.

Whatever the availability of jobs for women after the war, the fact remained that new walls had been breached, new options had been opened. As peacetime industries developed after the war, so did job opportunities with them. Secretarial positions increased, social service agencies opened, modeling and advertising agencies grew, publishing companies burgeoned, nondegreed nurse's aide positions multiplied. Women no longer thought of themselves as having only two options in life — teaching or nursing — or two definitions of self — married or religious. Imagination soared. Women began to think in terms of "careers," rather than simply of home life. Religious life was now only one of many things a woman could do. And she could make money doing them, as well.

The availability of money flowing out of the economic development of postwar society was no small factor in the emerging presence of women in society. After the war, the new middle class found itself safeguarded for the first time in history by rising wages, fair labor standard acts, the protection of unions, and the kind of retirement opportunities that rising social security funds and pension plans now made possible. Families even had enough money to educate their daughters as well as their sons. Now the country was assured not only of a female labor force but of an educated labor force of women, as well.

Women began to go to college, to earn money, to stay single long enough to taste the fruits of independence, and to make decisions on every level.

The women who would come to convents out of an environment like that were a different breed of candidate. This generation had a sense of self no amount of formation in docility could ever completely suppress.

But there were other factors at work in the changing image of women as well. Even the music of the 1960s, Rock and Roll, with its unabashedly sexual content, unleashed in a young postwar generation the full force of the fast-rising human sexuality movement. Chastity for its own sake became debatable. The birth control pill, long promised and recently released, gave the women of the decade a whole new sense of liberation, both from childbearing and, more importantly perhaps, from the fear of it. The morality of chastity became one thing; the unquestionable ideal of it another.

With both girls and boys becoming sexually active at much younger ages and outside of marriage, the idea of a life of chastity became more a nonissue than a religious issue. The secular world touted birth control. The advertising world made it public conversation. The idea of sexual activity as sacred territory and the stuff of sacraments lost its power to persuade.

Sex had become mainstream, common. Chastity and its essential relation to religious life became less and less defining. Now respect for chastity was a choice, not the certain sign of a call to religious life and certainly not to be assumed of anyone. "I don't ask applicants anymore if they are committed to a lifetime of celibacy," a vocation director said in my presence. "I ask them how long it's been since they've had sexual relations. If they haven't been celibate for at least six months, I tell them that they shouldn't attempt religious life."

Clearly, the birth control pill brought the world to a turning point in human relations. But there was more to the problem of the value and role of sexual activity than simple biology and physical impulse. The human development movement of the 1950s had been long in preparing the world for a whole new approach to life itself.

Human development theory, once basically an exercise in the modes, strategies, and stages of human growth, became over the years more and more conscious of the possible negative effects of suppression, repression, and negation on the human maturation process. Self-sacrifice began to lose some of its cachet. At the time that religious manuals were still requiring young religious not to smell flowers or use body powders or hold babies in order to control the demands of the senses, the idea of deliberate denial of the goods of life for the sake of holiness became disputable.

Under the influence of such new theories of personal fulfillment, child-rearing practices changed, education changed, and the valorization of religious life as an ascetic discipline or devotion to submission changed too.

It was a turning point in the way the world viewed the religious vocation. What had been accepted as "the higher vocation" now became actually suspect in many circles. Psychologists and psychiatrists looked with a wary eye at anyone who lived the religious life or contemplated making a commitment to it. They explored a person's underlying motives for becoming a religious and found most of them questionable. They worked with professed religious and more often than not concluded that the convent was not just an obstacle to good mental health but might even be the cause of the breakdown. They considered sexual control abnormal and self-sacrifice destructive of the full development of the person. Even family doctors when treating religious began to trace physical ailments to the psychological duress they now associated with living the religious life.

So engrained had the negative or self-denying aspects of religious life become that an articulation of its other determining values — spiritual immersion, gospel vision, and good works — took years to rejuvenate theologically. For people on the brink of making life choices, however, the thought of giving up what they now considered natural, normal, even a necessary part of the human growth process, became, for the first time in Catholic history, highly questionable.

More than that, under it all lurked two other realities: in the first place, the world was becoming a global community and, in the second, bringing the wisdom of the East to challenge the world of the West and the Christian theologies that drove it. For the first time in Western history, the thought and practices of Zen Buddhism, Islamic Sufism, and Hindu swamis became common spiritual currency. Now not only were there ways of life to choose between, there were radically other ways of thought to contend with as well. Thomas Merton, Trappist monk and author from Kentucky, went to the East, and Eastern thought became a factor in religious life.

Clearly, change begins a long time before change happens in a society, and it takes an even longer time before a new paradigm, a new way of viewing the world, becomes common coin. But that does not make the dis-ease any easier to understand, any simpler to come to grips with. On the contrary.

By the time Alice Schierberl became prioress in 1958, a number of novices and candidates of the period, young women who had grown accustomed to the personal freedom and public options a postwar world promised, had come to the community, lived the life for a while, and left. None of them were interviewed to determine why wholehearted and generous girls would take such a major step, enter a religious order with all the public attention that implied at that time, and then, only months later, make an equally major decision to leave the community with all the embarrassment and sense of failure that still implied. Theoretically, a girl had five years in which to make a final decision whether or not to remain in religious life forever. In reality, however, the very act of entering a community had become tantamount to a public commitment. So, to leave the convent, at any time — either before or after final profession — ranked tantamount to divorce in an age and a tradition that did not permit divorce, considered it a disgrace, saw the people who did it wanting in character. Many a young woman bore the scar of it for life.

To those with ears to hear, the very fact that more and more people were beginning to leave religious life under these conditions should have sounded a warning signal of things to come for religious life. But, in the first place, the institution was immutable, wasn't it? And in the second place, ironically, larger groups of candidates than normal kept entering. As a result, in the end, few, if anyone, heard the claxon. Life went on as business as usual except that business as usual was now long gone. The plain fact is, then, that when Alice Schierberl became prioress everything looked as it had always looked, except that it wasn't. At the same time, Sister Alice was younger herself than the prioresses before her had been. She brought youth and the understanding of youth into the office with her. She had intuitions and expectations of her own. But like most other women of that same period, they were as conflicted as they were visionary.

The proof of the situation lies in the way she administered the community, some days with great vision and openness, other days with strict adherence to past rules and values. Caught between two cultures, Alice's administration exposed the fault line between the medieval and the modern mind where religious life was concerned.

4

The Myth of Immutability

WHERE DID WE EVER get the idea in the first place that religious life was not only historically universal but also
structurally immutable? The question unmasks the power of
immutables everywhere. Hannah Arendt, the American political philosopher, wrote once, "The most radical revolutionary
will become a conservative on the day after the revolution."[2]
Few thinking social scientists would disagree. The human
enterprise has long lain in building our kingdoms in one phase
of our lives and then defending those kingdoms from all other
possibilities for the rest of our lives. Whatever the prevailing
myths about the persistent presence of change, the truth may
well be that change as a social constant is only now, in our
own century, becoming common.

Tradition and custom, habit and fixity have held sway in all
the major human institutions for hundreds, in some cases even
thousands, of years. The university system is much the same
now as it was in the year 1200. Western marriage forms have
remained largely identical in the course of Western civilization.
Religious rituals and creeds have remained much the same.
There have, of course, been "adjustments and adaptations."
But very little real change. Change, what the social scientist
Robert Nisbet defines as "a succession of differences in time
in a persisting identity,"[3] the notion that what we are dealing
with today is clearly unlike what it has been at an earlier time,
has been more rare than common. The nation-state is a change

in polity from tribal government. But the choice of a bicameral legislature over a national assembly is at best an adjustment. Air travel is a distinct change from sailing vessels. But two-seater bikes are simply adaptations of the unicycle. Bringing students to a monastery for an education is an adaptation of cloistered life to semicloistered life. Creating a monastic life where the members live and pray together while they work in the public arena is a change in the nature of what has normally been thought of as the monastic life. In every example of change, there is a "persisting identity" — transportation, governance, religious life. But there are, as well, deep differences in each of them.

The tendency of a static society is to make minor adaptations in basic structures to accommodate new cultural patterns without ever having to change the fundamental model. Schools allowed for separate grades as the number of pupils increased, for instance, but it was years before they went into nongraded education or abandoned the lecture model of teaching. Monasteries and convents extended themselves from one area to another as adjuncts of a parish society that replicated the schedule and lifestyle of the parent community. Only after Vatican II did it become common for individual religious to go separately to work with nonparish groups in public areas.

In each case, fundamental changes in outlook and purpose began to permeate what had been rigidly structured groups for rigidly defined purposes. The question is why adaptation persists when change is clearly needed to meet the changing circumstances around it. Why doesn't change happen more often?

There are multiple explanations for the persistence in time of outdated behaviors. Lack of social contact is surely one of them. Communities separated by the Alps, for instance, plowed the same fields, ate the same food, cooked the same meals, wore the same style clothes, and did the same chores the same way, though often differently than their neighbors, for hundreds of years.

Lack of communication systems is certainly another barrier to the emergence of new developments. Prior to the technological expansions of the twentieth century, immediacy simply had no meaning. It could take fifty years for an idea to circle the globe, let alone light down in place after place at the same time, like yoga from India being taught in California.

Lack of travel opportunities was obviously a third obstacle to change. Roland Warren argues that in the 1930s in the United States the average person still traveled on an average only seven miles from their homes annually. Until a traveler appeared bringing the first pair of sheep from outside the country, no sheep grazed on American mountains, no fences were designed to keep them out, no cattle wars began, no new territories developed.

Change was a foreign country; immutability reigned as a given in almost every facet of life.

In religious life, the concept of changelessness lingered most fixed of all. After all, this arena had been marked sacred ground. Here change was unthinkable. This arena lay outside the pale of human intervention. God was changeless, after all. And so were the things connected to God, religious life one of them and women's religious life a chief example. Women's lives everywhere and anywhere were basically static, hedged around by common prescriptions. And women's religious life, more than most, had been defined into canon law.

Law, however, is no guarantee of anything social. Once law fails to serve the needs of the governed, that law is not long for this world. If not changed, it will be subverted. If not subverted, it will be ignored. Social norms like love of country or property laws that advantage males or constitutional prescriptions that count slaves as two-thirds of a legal person or deny the vote to women are learned values, not absolutes. They are designed to enable a group to meet its felt needs. When those needs change or those standards fail, those norms change too.

In Austria, at the Benedictine abbey of Nonnberg in Salzburg, during a tour of American Benedictine prioresses to those European monasteries that had given rise to American foundations,

I discovered the truth of social fixity and its relation to my own life. Salzburg, founded in 700, was the motherhouse from which the community at Eichstatt had come in the eleventh century. Eichstatt was the community from which the foundation in Erie had come eleven hundred years later. In Salzburg I noticed, unlike the other communities we had visited, the rings worn by the nuns in this community were exactly the same as our own. "Do you have any idea where this ring came from?" I asked the archivist, pointing at mine and gesturing toward hers. "I certainly do," she said back quickly, with the slightest ring of indignation in her voice. "It came from here. The drawings for it are in the archives." I raised my eyebrows. "Really?" I said. "Do you know when?" Since Erie was founded in 1856, I calculated that the design that obviously had to have come from Europe with our original sisters might well have been over 150 years old. "The ring was cast in the 1300s," she said.

The ring had been drawn almost seven hundred years after the origin of the community and almost seven hundred years before I asked the question. With palm fronds around the band and IHS imposed on the cross, it had been used for seven hundred years to illustrate the paschal mystery to which the Benedictine life is meant to point. It was an idea firmly fixed in the formation of a Benedictine woman: those who follow Christ will rise with him. That willingness to follow Christ obviously implies both death and resurrection — resurrection into eternal life, certainly, but death to the self and the world with, as the prayer implied, "all its pomps and lures." The idea of immutability was built right into the symbols of the life. It was part of the air we breathed.

Standards such as these do not change easily. Religious ideals, we were sure, based as they were in the spiritual, the mystical, the mysterious, remained immutable while everything around them changed. Galileo became the archsymbol of the tension between the immutables of the spirit and the process of human development. The whole idea that the universe did not revolve around "man," God's highest creature, but that instead the earth revolved around the sun attacked the very foundations of the theology of creation. Galileo found himself threatened with excommunication, his work denounced — telescope or no telescope, proof or no proof. It took centuries for the idea of the heliocentric universe to find reconciliation in both science and theology.

Now, in the mid-twentieth century, the idea of death to self was a religious ideal being seriously examined by modern American society. New fields of science, especially psychiatry and psychology, were especially hostile to the idea. A new social theory, communism, branded concepts such as that the work of oppressors and the theology of slaves. Economic development gave a new kind of freedom that encouraged the "good life" and "having it all." To the public mind, death to self was no longer something to be either sought or accepted. "Neurotic," "unhealthy," such ideas were called now. The implications of such a position for the credibility of religious life and its attractiveness to the women of such a culture became more important by the day as secular education emphasized life while religious structures militated against it.

And yet it was not the first time that religious life — even the Benedictine life that had found root in Erie over a hundred years earlier — had known wrenching change. The mere move from ancient, established, cloistered abbeys in Germany to the wilds of a Pennsylvania forest had already reshaped the life once.

Here, the new young community in Erie lived in small frame houses, not in great palatial bastions of religious seclusion common in a Europe many of whose monasteries had developed as royal estates. The very physical changes necessary to survive in the teeming, unsettled areas of the United States, let alone the fierce independence of American culture and the needs of German-Catholic immigrants in an English-Protestant society, began to erode centuries of old patterns.

The cloisters — that separation by distance, walls, and grille that had long marked cloistered convent life — disappeared, if for no other reason than that no one could afford to build them here, and what's more, the nuns were teaching children right in the middle of their own limited living space. It was too late to think about grilles and walls now. The sisters, after all, had come to serve German immigrants, to teach their children the faith, to provide a Catholic enclave for them in an often suspicious, if not hostile, Protestant world. That meant doing those things when and where and how they could in the environment that existed here, not in Germany.

The daily schedule changed to allow for public service. Getting up in the middle of the night for vigils was impossible if they were to spend their days teaching small children.

The professional advancement of community members became a given as the need to meet state standards in education increased. Over the years, the community's relation to seculars and secular functions like professional conferences and college courses took on a never-before-experienced priority.

Most important of all, perhaps, here in the United States the government — fiercely separated from any kind of organized religious activity — did not provide financial support for religious life as it had in Germany. Here, in a secular society built on the absolute separation of church and state, religious had to provide for themselves. And that changed everything.

The tension between what had been for centuries the norms of the life and what had become a whole new way of being "religious" in the New World created a kind of live-and-lurch mentality that made negotiating the here and now a daily problem, a kind of spiritual schizophrenia that we began to see as normal. Yes, we were Benedictines from Eichstatt; no, we did not live exactly the same way our forebears in Eichstatt did because we lived and worked under very different circumstances.

Nevertheless, though we ourselves in our generation had never lived the European mode of Benedictine life for women that our ancestors did, it was clear to us that there was some kind of "standard" out there, an archetype, to which we apparently aspired but could now never really reach. We lived between two models of the life, one "pristine," we thought;

the other necessary but beyond us. Trying to live the gospel in a new cultural environment seemed to make us less Benedictine. The struggle was to choose between the two. How could we be the "Benedictines" we said we were and serve the society we said we had come to serve. The struggle came from the fact that we made every attempt to do both.

We went on trying to keep "cloister" when the strict concept of cloister was not only long gone but even potentially destructive of the ministries we were trying to perform. We worked with laypeople daily but created "visiting days" for families, for instance, and relegated them to the edges of our lives. We never left the monastery grounds by ourselves, even to go out to a doctor's appointment. "Traveling companions" — the custom of assigning one sister to go with another one to meetings or appointments — maintained the notion of our separateness from "the world," as well as assured our security. We never worked in our classrooms on Saturday without asking on our knees each and every time for permission to go there to do the work we were obliged to do. We never called our parents on a phone or walked out of the convents in which we lived onto the main street of the town or went to chapel during the day or ate an orange outside of mealtime without permission.

We lived in one mental world and made little careening attempts to live in another one, the real one. We went through life getting "permission" to do what we had been told to do so there would be no doubt that with all our professional competence or independent expertise we were still humble, still "obedient."

As a result, the system roiled with tension. Only the theology of asceticism and the promise of heavenly reward and the notion of responding to a "higher vocation" by living this way held it together as the world around it moved steadily on. We began to confuse the moral, the immoral, and the amoral. We made holiness out of the most mundane of behaviors and left the really moral questions of society to someone else. We taught the gospel but we saw no obligation to speak to it ourselves.

Then, in 1963, change of the degree that took us out of one ancient religious culture in Germany in 1852 to a modern culture in the United States began to happen again.

It was at just such a crossover moment in time that Sister Alice Schierberl became the youngest prioress in the history of the community. Elected in 1958 at the age of thirty-eight, she was a bridge between two generations. She was born just as women were getting the vote, just as the Great War that had engulfed all of Europe was ending, just as papal infallibility and the implications of that concept for the changelessness of the church in a world on the brink of change had become common currency. She came to office just as women were beginning to function in the professions, just as Pius XII opened scripture to professional research, just as the Western world settled down to battle communism. It was a world in flux. It was deeply conservative in some aspects, stirring with promise of change in others. And religious life existed in the middle of it, more and more out of touch every day, shaped in one culture but attempting to live and serve in a newly emerging other one.

The question is, What kind of religious life did Alice Schierberl inherit and what did she do with it?

Part Two

Deconstruction

The real problem with change is that it means the undoing of what went before it. That kind of revisionism is hard enough in the business world where people come and go between one job and another, between the office and a family life somewhere else. It is even harder when it involves the sensitivities of a living community, all of whose members have lived the past for varying degrees of time, in varying intensities, with varying measures of similarity between life as they knew it before they entered the convent and life as they went on living it there.

The renewal of religious life did not simply involve a community's willingness to adopt a checklist of new behaviors. It required that religious cease to do a number of things that had been considered eternal, thought of as absolutes, once assumed were the ultimate norms of sanctity. Renewal, suddenly, harked back to the author of Ecclesiastes who wrote simply but profoundly, "There is a time for tearing down and a time for building up."

The first task of renewal, though we hardly knew it then, called for the courage to tear things down, to eliminate those rituals, customs, works that were no longer effective. The destruction of public image and internal certainties that followed seemed as endless as the absolutes that had preceded them: "I'm not leaving religious life," I told my parents when I announced after months of turmoil that I would not be staying

*in the community much longer. "Religious life is leaving me."
It had been a stormy year, full of uncertainty, rife with strain.
The remark was a wail for a lost life, not a victory cry.*

*Renewal, we did not realize then, required more than cre-
ativity. It required, first of all, that we dismantle much of our
old ways of looking at life, of looking at ministry, of looking
even at the self. Renewal, ironically, required deconstruction.*

*The most difficult part of any change, perhaps, lies in real-
izing that the beliefs that brought us and our enterprise to this
moment in time have changed. Discovering that the structures
that had controlled the life — the ways we used to do things —
are no longer effective strikes at the very roots of the system.
Admitting that the goals of the group, the reasons for which
the group had come together in the first place, are no longer
valid, no longer valued, can be enough to take the spirit right
out of the soul of a group. Then the very viability of the venture
comes into question. Religious life suffered from all three.*

*Nearly all religious who went through renewal remember
the first time it dawned on them that the religious vocation
was just one more vocation in an array of possible paths to
God, not better, not worse, just normal. We had been told for
so long that a religious vocation was a "higher" vocation that
"normal" was tantamount to failure.*

*They know, too, how it felt to find themselves without the
nice, warm, protective system of "assignments." Someone else
decided what they would do, where they would live and with
whom, as well as what grade they would teach or work they
would do. Difficult as the assignment system might have been,
it had nevertheless brought with it a kind of security. It in-
sured religious against job loss, against rejection, even against
the social responsibility to make themselves liked or needed or
wanted.*

*They remember, as well, how it felt to watch community
members leave schools to begin other ministries. Teaching in
parochial schools had been the definition of religious life for
as long as they could remember. No treasons could have been
more treasonous to the life than leaving it.*

Yes, all those things were necessary if religious and laity were to be able to work together for the reign of God. Yes, finding ways to maximize their talents was a necessary part of self-development. Yes, religious were needed now by whole other parts of society. But realizing that some kind of change is needed and knowing exactly what has to be put down, to end, to stop, in order to make the kinds of change such change implies are two different things.

If truth were known, most people seldom really recognize when one thing has served its purpose and another needs to begin. Not if we're emotionally attached to it, not if it's "always been this way." But if a group in the throes of cultural change is to go on functioning with purpose and with vigor, new ideas have to be formulated, new goals chosen, new structures devised to make the new direction attainable. Otherwise, the group cannot really renew, however sincere its desire. Instead, it simply watches itself wind slowly down as one long-established element after another becomes less and less socially effective, less spiritually developmental, less personally attractive. Then, in the end, it doesn't change at all. It simply dies on the vine.

Of all the dimensions of change, old ideas are the most difficult to abandon. Those ideas form the ground on which we stand. They are the very foundation of our world. To move forward, therefore, a group must begin to recognize the new issues that the old ideas do not resolve. They have to look full front at the situations that the traditional assumptions on which they depend for their legitimacy hide from view. They have to reexamine everything they do and why they're doing it. They have to be willing to "deconstruct" what they have given a lifetime to internalizing.

Religious life — and the society in which it was immersed — held clear ideas about family, about theology, about women that posited one kind of world in a world that was clearly questioning, reexamining, deconstructing, all of them. At many levels yet, it is still in the midst of deconstructing them.

Women religious, we knew, were anonymous, invisible, and genderless creatures who lived only to serve Catholic schools and hospitals, though we knew at the same time that they existed long before either. Coming to understand that the accoutrements of religious life — the lifestyle, the dress, the customs — were simply remnants of earlier centuries, not sacred artifacts in themselves, left the world face-to-face with the question of whether religious life has any place in this century or not.

Now those ideas are the coin of the realm. In 1965, to the traditionalists around us for whom being medieval was of the essence of religious fidelity, they had all the earmarks of heresy.

Deconstruction is that moment in time when what we always accepted as the unassailable givens of life fail to withstand either the scrutiny of reason or the needs of the present. Then the old system begins to unravel. Then the ideas lose their power to compel. Then social change begins, whether people realize it or not.

Deconstruction is the shocking, heretical, initial phase of social change. It promises more than it can give. It does more than it can explain. It brings with it feelings of danger, excitement, hope, and disheartenment, all of which affect everybody at different times and at the same time always. It is the unchartered water in which a group finds itself almost accidentally, almost certainly unknowingly, with all the adventure — and the pressure — that implies.

5

Between Two Poles

S ISTER ALICE was a prioress caught at the crossroads of church and culture. The church remained adamant about its relationship to the world. The "world" was to be avoided. Catholicism was a world unto itself. The culture was suspect. Catholicism was unchangeable. The church was a world under siege. The culture, on the other hand, had, it seemed, turned upside down overnight.

Denominationalism remained, but now it was more private in tone than public. "Irish need not apply" signs were long gone, and Catholics were beginning to break through employment barriers, even in the professions, aided in large part, of course, by the system of Catholic education that had sprung up across the country from grade school through college almost entirely on the backs of teaching orders of nuns. Male religious orders taught mainly at the college level, and only a few of those groups accepted women students in any capacity.

The United States, now the strongest and wealthiest power in the Western world, was awash in the money made, but not spent, during wartime. Free now of military contracts, production levels of civilian commodities soared. Consumerism rose at unprecedented rates.

Old patterns began to change, imperceptibly at first, then in a cataclysm of new possibilities made both thinkable and doable by the wartime culture itself. The country became mobile. The automobile became a standard fixture at every level of society. Families bought cars and went on vacations and began to move around the country in search of peacetime jobs. Air travel crept into public consciousness. Even children began to go on "class trips" and camping trips. Old boundaries began to break down. Women's roles and public postures changed drastically from prewar norms.

Women in general were, for the most part, basically house-bound, largely family-centered in their interests, usually restricted in their movements, almost totally dependent on men for their sustenance and direction, and little involved in the public dimensions of life other than teaching or nursing. By 1960 women were beginning to appear everywhere. They drove cars and held public jobs too. They voted for public officials and developed interests in public affairs. They had money and spent it.

But change had passed the convents by — or convents allowed change to pass them by. Women in the monastery still seldom left the premises, hardly ever read newspapers, operated only in parochial schools and convent academies under strict schedules and controls, and depended totally on the monastery to supply even their most personal needs. Toothpaste, for instance, came from the community cupboard, bought by the community procurator. The smallest of decisions were made for them by someone else. And it showed. Dependence, called "obedience," had become a virtue.

In some ways, the implications of such a lifestyle weighed more heavily on Alice than on the community itself. Unlike most of the community, she herself had seen a world outside the world of the monastery. As a graduate student at Notre Dame in the late 1940s, she had talked to major public thinkers, mixed with people, gone places most other sisters never thought possible. Having had her own horizons expanded, she began to expand the worldview of those around her. As local superior in Oil City before her election as prioress, for instance, Sister Alice had substituted a radio news broadcast for the standard suppertime table reading fare from spiritual reading books. "You have to know what's going on in the world if you're going to teach it!" she declared one night as she set up the radio at the head of the table. "What's going on in the world is holy, too, you know," she said.

Alice had been among the first members of the community Mother Sylvester had sent en masse to some of the best colleges in the country. "From Sister Alice on down" had become a community mantra, in fact, a code that signaled a watershed in community life. Intent on raising the professional level of the community but strapped for the money to do it, Mother Sylvester had simply divided the community in half and begun to concentrate almost exclusively on the professional preparation of younger, newer members.

Sisters "from Sister Alice on down," were sent to conferences and cultural presentations and civic events. They were sent out of Erie to obtain master's degrees at the largest Catholic universities in the country. They saw a world beyond their tiny little convent world on East Ninth Street with its span of one block in one direction, half a block in the other. It was still a totally Catholic world, yes, but a far larger one, nevertheless, than they had ever known.

Slowly but surely, the apparently simple decision to concentrate on the professional education of the community for the sake of state certification of Catholic schools began as well to stretch the psychological and theological horizons of what had been a very self-contained, very theologically unprepared group.

Alice, now holder of a master's degree from the University of Notre Dame, was full of new ideas about church, about liturgy, about theology itself. And she was eager to make them real. She had the energy for it. She had the charisma for it. She had everything, perhaps, but the emotional endurance it would take to struggle with the implications of cultivating the future in an institution rooted in a theological past.

With her social boundaries widened by five years of summer school and the new worldview it had given her, Alice found herself steeped in the new horizons of one world but living in the confines of the one before it. Alice did not bear the brunt of the tension easily.

Every morning after breakfast, sisters lined up outside the prioress's office to ask for simple permissions: "For the love of Jesus, Mother," each of them said on the knees, "may I go to the eye doctor today?" "May I attend my cousin's funeral today?" "May I go to a lecture at a local college?" "May I get new shoes?" "May I write to a family friend?" The list went on hour after hour, day after day.

Sometimes the problems taken to the prioress's office were complaints, not requests for personal permissions. "Sister Somebody didn't fold the sheets correctly," one sister would tell about another. Or wash the dishes correctly, or distribute the mail correctly. Sister Somebody-else had broken night-silence. Sister Somebody needed to be corrected. What was the prioress going to do about such infringements of community discipline?

"I'll have to ask Mother" had become the driving force behind all the questions of a sister's day. Superiors, on the other hand, spent their nights answering them: making up lists of who should do table waiting, or table reading, or prayer leading, or phone duty every week and who should accompany whom to the doctors' offices in town every day and who should walk with whom in funeral processions. And, of course, they wrote a steady stream of letters of correction designed to make fast the customs of the house.

It didn't take too many months before it became clear that it was too much for a woman who walked through halls with her eyes up, not down, her elbows out and her scapular flying. Alice was free-form, not molded. And this life as it was lived now — half-cloistered, half not — was meant to mold people, superiors as well as sisters.

The strain of it didn't last long.

Alice's administration swung between the two poles of her own life: formation in the values of the past and, at the same time, formation in the vision of a freer, fuller future. And her emotions swung with them.

Sometimes her corrections were harsh and rigid. "Sisters, do NOT ask people to bring you work supplies. If you want something, ASK for it as you are supposed to." (Capital letters hers.) Her letters came with liberal amounts of underlining and a good many exclamation points. But at other times, she simply dispensed with custom completely and said over and over again, an edge to her voice, what came to be a community scripture: "Authority is commensurate with responsibility, Sisters. Don't ask me if you can go over to school. If you have work to do there, of course you must go!" The lesson got through despite the fact that the practice of it seemed often to be erratic.

Sometimes she kept the Customs Book rigorously and the isolation that went with it. "Sisters are not to drive in the front seat of a car with a man," one reminder read. "Not even with their fathers!" At other times, she was recklessly broad in her interpretations of religious commitment. When the mother of a young sister said to her, "What good is it if she can only come home when I die?" Alice called the practice a sin against filial piety. "That will end soon," she promised, though there wasn't a hint of it in the institutional air. Then, the next year she herself began the appeals to the federation that began the discussions that led, finally, to a change in the constitutions.

Alice was a contemplative at heart, totally reflective about everything she did. She lived in the scriptures, made them real, and expected the rest of the community to do the same. Prayer ceased to be simply part of the daily routine. The scriptures became the warp and woof of the day, written to us as living history, she taught us, rather than only as recorded history. To young sisters who were more inclined to concentrate on the sacrifices of the life rather than on its freedom of heart, she was especially fond of proclaiming, "This is the day the Lord has made, Sisters," and you were expected to answer back in full throat, "Let us be glad and rejoice therein!"

She abhorred dependence and found herself caught between the childlike underdevelopment of older sisters who had never been allowed to make an independent decision in their entire lives and an awareness of the maturation level of even young girls in postwar America. One day, chafing under the irritation of it, she burst out of the prioress's office, set up a card table with great fanfare, took an older sister by the hand and said, "Sister Agnes, those are stamps on that table. I'm not going to send your mail for you! Lick them yourself!" And from that day forward she never read a sister's outgoing mail again.

At the same time, she hired a music consultant from Manhattanville, who kept us in choir practice every day for hours, regardless of how the amount of time spent there might affect the rest of our schedule or, for that matter, our attitude toward choral prayer itself. She didn't like the way we sang the Divine Office, she said, so she saw to it that we sang nothing but the Divine Office for hours, no excuses accepted, no exceptions condoned. So much for personal decision-making. So much for authority being commensurate with responsibility. Benedictines sang the Office, and whatever else we did, we were going to do that well. Or else.

She worked hard and expected everyone else to do the same. No project was too large, no obstacles insurmountable. To plead impossibility to Alice was to be a "bawlbaby."

Prayer time and periods of *lectio divina* were for sitting and thinking. All other times were for work, much of it in manual labor — which made it even harder to stay awake during *lectio*. She was famous for thinking up the wrong jobs for the wrong people at the wrong time. One sister had to plant the same tree four times until she got it right. She had another group lay down and take up a stone walk from the old farmhouse to the creek three times. They baked in the hot sun in the long habits they worked in until she was satisfied with the angle of the path.

At the same time, I remember her calling to me when I was a young nineteen-year-old junior-professed, bucket in hand, to put it down and walk with her for a moment. "Here," she said, slipping a copy of Sertilange's *The Intellectual Life* quietly under my scapular. "Read that. You are going to need it." And I did.

That book changed my life as, in fact, those penetrating, insightful, charismatic, and erratic actions of hers, in the end, changed the community's future as well.

6

When Cultures Collide

A LICE WAS NOT so much a woman of contradictions as she was a woman who lived in a culture of contradictions. The church was going one way, the world another. People of vision, and she was one of them, knew that the fissure between the two needed to be reconciled. The question was how that could possibly be done when you were living in both and saw the values of both as well. How could that be done when you were a superior who saw the necessity of one thing but were responsible for maintaining the other?

Sister Alice wanted a community made up of religious women, women religious, not adult children, a perspective that would eventually demand a whole new theology of obedience different from the way it was then being lived. The tensions of negotiating between the two were only too clear. She could give a person great latitude and allow that person even greater experiences. At the same time, she could take it all back, directing the publication of a high school yearbook or a liturgical event or a sister's daily schedule from her own bedroom. She was obviously confused about her own role and her confusion confused us. But her personal Customs Book, found years later, lay riddled with X-marks through every page. "Nonsense!" she wrote next to some items. "Ridiculous!" next to others. Most pages simply carried a large X through them from one corner to another to signify that none of those things would ever be done in the Erie community again.

At the end of her six-year term, worn down by the contradictions of it all, worn out by the mysterious illness that plagued her, overmedicated and undertreated, the night before what would ordinarily have been her second election, she withdrew her name from the list of eligible nominees.

It had been a tumultuous time, a great ride, a hard six years in many ways — both for her and for a community ever unsure of what the next moment would bring in her — but, even more, it was a groundbreaking period of major proportions. She left the community a legacy that became the bridge to a whole new period of religious life. And she left it despite the price she paid for it in both physical and emotional health. In fact, maybe if she had been completely physically and emotionally well, she might never have been able to do it. After all, it is the "reasonable" that gives bad law too much respect. As a result, her clear perception of the situation she was in and the toll it took on people, starting with herself, perhaps, led her to strike out in new directions, whatever the price she had to pay from visitators or bishops or retreat directors or even community members themselves for the doing of it.

In the end, she gave new insight into the relationship between vision and institutional structures. Structures, we learned from her, were changeable. We knew that was true because we had seen her change them. In great sweeping instants, she wiped out the customs of years and replaced them with new ways of living and looking at life. And she did it while those structures were, at least theoretically, still in place, still the law of the religious landscape.

She paved the way, too, for a religious life made up of strong women who carry within themselves the reasons for their commitment, rather than of child-nuns who look to a mother to tell them what to do. The very fact of her long, erratic illness made getting permissions largely impossible. She did not go to her office to give them. But life had to go on. So community members began to "presume permission" for things — a time-honored practice, at least in print — when the superior was unavoidably unavailable. In fact, during Alice's administration, "presuming permission" began to be the order of the day. If she noticed that she was being asked less and less as time went by, she never said anything. If we noticed that what had been one of the mainstays of the life had apparently washed way, we simply began to notice it less and less as time went on. We became more and more comfortable with doing what must be done simply because it had to be done.

She brought to the era a theology of community that would serve us well in later years when all the structures that had once defined the life — the habit, the customs, the work, even the former prayer schedule — were no longer in place. We were simply part of "the Communion of Saints," she taught us. We were there as part of the ongoing "cloud of witnesses" who had publicly committed ourselves to meeting the responsibility to bring the gospel to our own time. We were there, in other words, for more than keeping the rules or living a lifestyle or "giving up our own wills" so that we would then presumably be doing the "will of God." The gospel was the will of God for us, she taught us, and as the years went by what she meant by that teaching became more and more clear.

She made the liturgy a living, breathing part of life. Stretched by the lectures of Godfrey Diekmann, OSB, at Notre Dame and other great liturgical thinkers of her time, she set out to make Erie more a liturgical community than simply a praying community. She began to circulate the publication *Orate Fratres* — now *Worship* magazine — with its whole new awareness of the living liturgical year. And then she simply cleared the library shelves of years of pious devotional readings. "We're cleaning this place out," she told Sister Helen Heher. And she did. What up to now had been the basic spiritual fare of the community disappeared in one fell swoop to make room for volumes of liturgical spirituality that changed the entire spiritual vision of the community.

She lived for the day the Office would finally be said in English. Time and again the permission was promised and then withdrawn. When the indult finally came, Alice went to chapel as the prayer leader intoned the age-old Latin that had been the language of the Office for centuries. "*Jube domine, benedicere,*" Carolyn Gorny-Kopkowski chanted. "In English, in English," Mother Alice said aloud. And then and there, the language of community prayer changed. No preparation, no education, no preliminaries.

And all the time, she went on trying to balance a life of rigid rules with a new kind of spiritual dynamism. She paid a great price to do it.

The Second Vatican Council opened in 1962. A whole new church loomed on the horizon but not soon enough to liberate Alice from her commitment to the old as well as confirm her vision of the new. By 1963, emotionally depleted and physically weak, she began to withdraw more and more from the community. By 1964, with the council now beginning to produce documents that shocked the religious world with their openness and redefinitions, even of the church itself, the community found itself on the verge of another election. Alice did not present herself for consideration again. But no matter: her work had already been finished.

She had, in her own way, been harbinger of the church to come. Perhaps her greatest problem was that she was basically alone in announcing it. Alice had brought to the community respect for liturgical theology, a commitment to the adult feminine, an extension of the traditional military concept of obedience, authorization for intellectual as well as spiritual development, and a passion for change.

With all the things she did change, there was just as much that she did not change. She did not change the kind of government structures that were designed to be hierarchical. She did not change the herd mentality of religious life. She called for "adulthood" but really gave very little real freedom of choice. She did not change the role of the community in society. We went on living behind invisible walls, remote and detached from the world around us. She did not change the definition of the life. But she did, ironically, model a new one herself.

Alice left office in 1964 but, as unlikely as it may seem, she went on leading the community long after her term as prioress was over. Alice Schierberl became the first Benedictine sister of Erie to begin a direct outreach to the poor in inner-city Erie.

Religious life had deteriorated over time into a kind of personal devotion to personal salvation. Religious engaged in "social works" — especially those devoted to the development of the Catholic community — but these were basically extraneous to the notion of religious life itself, done on the side, in addition to the real purpose of religious life. The salvation of the self was key; the salvation of the world was not.

On the other hand, the liturgical life, Alice knew from the works of the Benedictine liturgist, Virgil Michel, involved living out the life of Christ here and now. Liturgy and social action were not opposing theologies, she learned. In fact, to be real, liturgy — the living of the life of Christ — demanded a commitment to social justice. This newly revived liturgical theology touched her deeply. She had taught it to high school students years before she became prioress. "What's happened in history is now happening in mystery, girls!" she taught. And "Sisters, we are to 'anticipate the needs of the saints,'" she taught from St. Paul, as they made food baskets for home delivery.

But most of all, she lived it herself for all to see.

In 1964, Sister Alice Schierberl left office as prioress and, with Sister Theophane, a past subprioress, high school administrator, and nurse, a thinker of immense proportions, moved into an old brick home in the middle of a black neighborhood where, as a community, we had never been before. From that spot in the center of the city, she washed and bathed the sores of Grandma Stewart every day, taught the women of the neighborhood how to clean, baked fresh food for them, and took care of the children. On my way to the library one day, she hailed me into a car with her, drove to a frame box of a house with peeling paint and small windows. The mother inside was groaning on a bare cot in the hot, dark front room.

"Here," she said to me, shoving a two-year-old black boy-child into my arms. "Take him over to the Home Ec lab, give him a bath in the sink, wash his clothes, and feed him. It will do you good."

I had grown up an only child, totally removed from small children, bewildered by the very sight of a needy baby and completely unprepared to help in any way. I took the child awkwardly and did just what I was told, clumsily, tentatively, reluctantly. But Alice was right; it did me good for the rest of my life. I never write or say a word to this day that I don't remember that quiet, crusty baby, too sick to cry, too hungry to eat, his head against my shoulder, his life in my untrained hands.

While we watched, Sister Alice went on to open the first daycare program in the center of the city in the community's former motherhouse. She worked with the local housing authority to build homes for the poor. She went into the fields to get the children of migrant workers into Head Start programs. She cajoled mayors and Rotary Clubs and churches to help her. And, most of all, she plagued the conscience of the Erie Benedictine Sisters themselves to go beyond our antiseptic conventual world, our too, too ordered lives, to be with the poor, to be the voice of the poor.

Alice was the beginning of the end of a religious life, half-medieval, half-modern, half-European, half-American, basically institutional and, by that time, only symbolically prophetic. Living under Alice had been unpredictable, at best, but it was also, in its own way, freshening. In Alice, medieval and modern religious life had met head on, neither one sure of the ongoing place of the other.

7

The Uncomfortable Cusp of Change

SOCIAL THEORISTS make a distinction between "change" and "adjustment." The evolutionary nature of institutions assumes a continual process of adjustment. For an institution to survive, it only makes sense that it must keep abreast of new ideas in the field. At the same time, simply upgrading a present process is seldom enough to assure the survival of an institution when the whole nature of the undertaking and the world around it changes.

Perhaps few other industries have changed so much in so short a time, for instance, as has the printing industry. Print shops began with the invention of movable metal type in the fifteenth century. The process continued basically unaltered far into the twentieth century. There were modifications to the industry, of course. Copper plate photography, for instance, made the printing of pictures possible and the foot pedal that drove the press became motorized someplace along the line. Over the years, printing companies continued to grow and develop simply by moving to larger type beds, plastic coated halftones, automatic-feed printers. Everything looked new, perhaps, with the introduction of the new equipment, but the fact remains that adjustments got made within a given frame of reference. Books were published by spreading ink over type and pressing it onto single sheets of paper. No one doubted that. It never crossed most people's minds that it could be done any other way.

Then, suddenly, half-tone photography and lithographic plates were invented. The use of this new type of printing process, totally devoid of movable type and hand-fed printing platens, gave way to oil-base inks and water on a metal plate on a motor-driven machine. And as the changes came, a good many printers tried to survive by converting their hand-fed platens and movable-type processes to motor-driven presses. But the new world could not be held off.

Printers who wanted to stay in printing were forced to accept an entire change of process, a whole new way of looking at the world of lithographic arts.

Now the move from that process to digital cameras and computerized desktop publication requires an even greater leap into an unknown technology. Each of the stages demands a new way of thinking, new skills, new services, new learning. Each of them requires change.

Multiple adjustments could be made within each of those systems, of course (larger paper sheet size, new cutting machines, different sheet feed mechanisms) but change — real change — came with the adoption of another whole world-view about the nature and process of printing. The need to change in order to compete, the need to change in order to stay exactly what they were, ended many a flourishing printing business. And not printing businesses only. There is no record of how many companies were able, for instance, to convert from making horse buggies to making Model T Fords.

No, change is not "adjustment"; change turns the world as we know it on its axis.

Faced with the need to change, many temporize. Some resist. A few attempt and fail. But in the end, the change is always decisive, if not for this generation, certainly for the next.

So the question is, Why, if change is inevitable in the face of new theory and new thought, is change so difficult?

The answers are many. For some people, the whole effort of beginning a major work all over again seems, at one stage or another of life, to demand more energy than they have to give. They choose simply to live the old way out. For others, change

implies a betrayal of the values of the past. What their ancestors built, they feel obligated to maintain. For even more, the
need to change erodes personal confidence and introduces confusion about what is fluid and can change and what needs to be
changed but can't be changed, about what are basics and what
are options, about what is fidelity and what is faithlessness.
Then change becomes a moral question.

The problems of change in the institutional world are
myriad. What structures must be maintained at all cost if the
group is to be able to go on functioning well? Here the question is functionality. The problems of change in the theological
arena, on the other hand, are of the essence of mystery. Here
the question is fidelity. What ideas must be maintained at all
cost if the group is to remain true to itself? Each challenge
presents its own struggles.

A shift in structures dislocates individuals. When structures
change, some positions are lost, many positions are changed.
More than that, role definitions shift and with them an entire set of human relationships. It becomes unclear who is in
charge of what and why.

The concept of "rank" — the ordering of the community in
terms of the entrance dates of each member — determined a
sister's entire life. A "younger" sister — no matter how chronologically old she was — was one who entered after you did and
so, the Customs Book said, she was, for instance, to allow
you to go through doorways before her. As a result, when
the concept disappeared in religious communities, years of
identity-building went with it. This ordering of the community
in the most minute ways — where they sat in chapel, where
they walked in procession, where they ate in the dining room,
who would be the automatic leader of a task group — gave role
clarity and created personal expectations as well. I remember
that on the day we entered the community we were led into
the community refectory in single file. I was at the very end
of the line. As the youngest member of this new group of postulants, that was my "rank." The community's pre–Vatican II

constitutions were clear about it: "Rank shall be assigned according to the time and age of entrance." But, even at that age, as I watched the shadows of the postulants in front of me play along the walls of the narrow halls, I thought to myself, a bit ruefully, it seems now, "I am going to be following this group around for the rest of my life."

Rank was a simple structure but it distinctly and quickly affected the sense of self and predicted a future direction. Not surprisingly then, it was one thing to be at the end of the line when the concept changed; it was surely another to be at the head of the line but find yourself in charge of, in command of, no one and nothing after years of being assured that the progression would be automatic.

When structures change, people lose a sense of who they are and what they do and how they do it. The emotional cost of structural change can hardly be calculated and can sometimes never be healed. People who lose their life employment because of "downsizing" in institutions are still left with the question of what was wrong with them that they were the people whose positions were eliminated rather than someone else's.

A shift in theory or theology is even more wrenching. Here the very issues of life and meaning, of why we do what we do, come into play.

The social norms, the beliefs and assumptions that identify, drive, and unite a group, are not merely window dressing. At least they don't start out that way. They form the matrix that brings a person to a group and the magnet that keeps them there.

People join groups that echo their own beliefs and desires, that give promise to their continuing support, that guarantee their expression and their constancy. When women entered religious life, they were told that they had chosen a "higher" vocation, that asceticism was its currency, and that they would receive "a hundredfold" in the next life for having done it. After Vatican II, they were told that there were no such things as "higher" and "lower" vocations, that what they had done all their lives, however difficult — however distasteful — was not necessary to sanctity and that, furthermore, could even now be actually harmful to the church.

The theological developments that came with Vatican II completely changed the worldview of the church. More than that, they changed the very nature and structures of religious life. The renewal of religious life was not an exercise, an "adjustment" of lifestyle. Renewal struck at the very foundations of the life. Vatican II presented religious life with a "paradigm shift" of immense proportions. Just as Galileo's assertion that the earth moved around the sun, not the sun around the earth, dislodged the notion of man's total superiority to all the rest of creation and shook the theological foundation of a cosmology that had been built on it for centuries, so did the theology of Vatican II completely upend the rationale for a religious commitment that had deteriorated into mystique, withdrawal, dependence, and triumphalistic denominationalism, however well-intentioned those things might have been.

When structures are in flux but ideas are stable, there is room for error. When ideas are in flux but structures are stable, there is room for confusion. But when both ideas and structures are in flux at the same time, error and confusion are of the order of the day. Vatican II brought both structures and ideas into flux.

Mary Margaret Kraus was barely in office when both things began to happen at once.

8

The Beginning of the End

THE SECOND VATICAN COUNCIL in 1962, as opposed to the First Vatican Council in 1869, completely changed the worldview of the church. Where Vatican I had concentrated on modern heresies and declaring the infallibility of the pope, Vatican II opened the church to the gifts and insights of the entire church and declared the need for the wisdom of all its members. It was a heady time, an exciting time, a turbulent time.

As documents came pouring out of the council in Rome, expectancy became the order of the day. People rushed to newspapers to find scraps of promise, bits of warning about what was going to happen next. The Catholic world entered the realm of possibility, and with it every other Christian church as well. Daughters and sons of the first reformation, they hoped for the success of this one, so the scandal of division could cease, so Christianity could be made whole again, so the gospel could be proclaimed with a common voice.

The hopes of the world were not disappointed. There was a new ring to the language of these new Roman documents, a new tone to the words. Rather than exhortation and a list of things that were forbidden, this council brought a list of ideals and the things that could be accomplished. Instead of corrections, the church got inspiration. Rather than emphasizing what was forbidden, this council raised up image after image of what should be done to be an effective part of a world on the brink of change. The church was calling the church to be its best self, its whole self.

Suddenly, being Catholic began to mean something new. Gone were the meatless Fridays that had marked Catholic populations for centuries. Gone were head coverings for women in church and all the implications of unworthiness that lurked under the practice. Gone was the Latin Mass. Gone was the medieval pomp and circumstance.

But being a woman religious in the heart of that church began to mean even more than the loss of cultural incidentals. For the average Catholic, Vatican II was a new way of thinking about church, faith, the world. For women religious, however, Vatican II meant a whole new way of living, of relating, of being in the world.

The last possibility became the greatest struggle of all. For women whose entire adult lives had revolved around withdrawing from the world, learning to be in it again demanded an entirely new repertoire of behaviors and skills and relationships and sense of purpose.

Anyone with an eye to social psychology or an overview of history would have known immediately how long and how hard the road ahead was bound to be. Life patterns were at stake. Social norms were at stake. Identity was at stake. Belief itself was at stake.

We should have known, perhaps, but caught in the vortex of the greatest spiritual change in centuries, few did.

Having been making adjustments for years now, thanks to Alice and her penchant for maturity, it all seemed to be about continuing the process of making necessary alterations to what had become a stilted way of living. But the days of adjustment were long gone. This period would be about change, about theological upheaval, about that dangerous moment in the human journey when the old road runs out and a new one has yet to be laid.

At first glance it seems that the document on the renewal of religious life that came out of the council was at best benign. It makes no major theological pronouncements. It sets no sights and gives no directives. It requires simply that women religious examine their lives according to "the charism of the order, the needs of the members and the signs of the times." If you were reading quickly, you could miss the sentence entirely. Even if you were reading slowly, in 1965 you were likely to miss the implications of it. The implications of the statement, in fact, were really embedded in the concepts contained in the other fifteen documents of Vatican II. To live in the heart of the church, to be as effective in the church of the future as they had been in the past, religious had to be in touch not simply with the document written directly to them but with every other document as well. After all, the lives of women religious were as deeply touched by the other documents as they were by their own. They worked with bishops and priests, with laity and liturgy, in this Christian country and in non-Christian countries too. They taught Catholicism and so they had to know it. If this was the new Catholicism, their own renewal depended on dealing with all of it, not just isolated facets of it. Otherwise how could they even begin to test the charism of the order and the signs of the times in this society, let alone the needs of the members in the doing of them.

The whole project would, at first glance, appear to be quick and clear.

But there were issues beyond the theological to be considered that would only make renewal even more difficult. To all intents and purposes, religious life had never been more successful. Novitiates across the country were teeming with new members. The Erie Benedictines themselves had been getting novices in greater numbers than at any time in history. The Catholic school system was expanding to the new suburbs in record numbers and young parishes called for sister-teachers to staff all the new schools that followed. Catholic dioceses had been in a building frenzy since the early 1960s.

The Catholic population, too, had grown in numbers and in wealth. There was a new stratum of Catholic professionals on the scene whose personal aspirations had soared but, more than that, who wanted something different for their children. It was a subtle shift, but an important one in the struggle between renewal and recommitment to the past. The greatest hope a parent held for a child now was not the priesthood or religious life. It was a college education and the promise it gave of the good life. Not in the next world. Here and now.

College enrollments swelled. Small Catholic colleges grew in stature and in size. And with those increases, novitiates began to decrease. It wasn't that Catholic families were any less Catholic. It was just that they had ceased to believe that being a good Catholic meant getting less, doing less, and being less than everybody else. Negative asceticism, withdrawal, self-sacrifice were no longer common spiritual ideals. Like everyone else in society, Catholics had been touched by the human sexuality movement, the human development movement, economic security, and, for women, the first stirrings of the feminist critique of society.

Suddenly, though large numbers of young women continued to come to religious life, just as many left. Clearly what they found there did not satisfy, did not inspire, did not compel. Between 1962 and 1982, in the span of one generation, more young women left than entered. Nor did the decline end there.

What was it that was lacking and what was it that was required and what happened to the community itself during that time?

9

The Silent Revolution

To understand the struggles of religious to renew a lifestyle, much of which had begun in the Middle Ages and all of which had been cast in stone by church law through the years, it is necessary to understand the ideal toward which they were striving. The documents of Vatican II were a call to the entire church to be church differently, in ways both truer to the gospel and more significant to the world. The documents of Vatican II, then, were both a beacon and an end toward which contemporary religious life would have to steer if the "renewal" programs they undertook would do anything more than make cosmetic adjustments in a time and in a church that needed change. The world around the church was plunging headlong into a crossover moment in time, after which nothing could possibly ever be the same again. The signs were clear: either the world and the church would change or the trends of the day would lead the world into social chaos and human cruelty on scales never before imagined and leave the church a memory of laughable irrelevance.

Four major issues converged in the postwar West: rampant nuclearism, creeping globalism, religious pluralism, and feminism. Each of them brought challenges to a world made smaller every day with the coming of new technologies the likes of which the world had never seen.

The end of the world had been created and was being stored in cornfields in Kansas and mountains in the Mongolian desert. Questions about who and what would control nuclear energy, nuclear power, and nuclear conflict plagued every major government and people on earth. Worse, the very morality of weapons such as these had yet to be pronounced upon by the church. The church that could condemn the birth control pill and condoms had said nothing about the Christian attitude toward nuclear weapons. The theological soundness of things like the just war theory in a nuclear world began to be debated and reviewed. Could there possibly be such a thing as a just war in a nuclear world? Who would discuss the question? Who would decide?

Globalism, the spreading tendency of large international corporations to control the resources, markets, labor forces and ecology of the rest of the world, now dominated the economic scene, leaving whole populations without either their resources or, at very least, the fruits of their labor. And all of it was beyond the rule of international law. Missionary orders who had once gone into foreign lands simply to evangelize the natives or support Catholic populations there found themselves in increasingly politicized situations. What was the Christian missionary duty now, to "obey legitimate authority" or to take the side of the local poor?

Colonialism, whatever its suppression of peoples, had also led to the integration of peoples. Rich and poor of every country, now English-speaking and English-educated, followed corporations around the world in large numbers, seeking jobs, looking for food. As a result, old regionalisms with their common language and common religions gave way to streams of new immigrants, refugees from the desertification of whole parts of the globe and victims of new low-intensity wars waged by puppet nations for the sake of either American or Russian interests.

Religious pluralism became the norm, especially in the West. Muslim mosques, Hindu temples, Buddhist shrines, Jewish synagogues all found a home in the heart of Christianity as well as in their native lands. How were these peoples to be related to in a pluralistic world? With civil rights, of course, but what was the implication of that theologically? After all, the Christian churches themselves were only beginning to put down their swords, to interact, and that cautiously. What was to be done now that Buddhists and Hindus, Jains and Sikhs had begun to build their own religious shrines and temples in a country bounded by oceans and accustomed to being a world unto itself? Was the church required to convert these people, to control them, to ban them, or to learn from them? Were religious to be defenders of the faith or developers of the faith?

Feminism, too, had arrived on the scene full blown and un-nuanced. Questions of reproductive health as well as debates about the "natural" role of women and the place of women in the church itself dominated the public arena. Whose body was a woman's body and where did that line end? Why were women not also being ordained? The country, led by the church, found itself polarized over these topics more than over nuclear war or globalism's new corporate slavery. The church remained adamantly opposed to all women's questions. "God has spoken, the question is closed," the church implied. "Who said so?" women demanded to know.

Women religious found themselves squarely in the middle of the problem, committed to human life but living the oppression that went with being a woman even in the church. More than that, they worked with poor women who, having been left to cope alone with the children men would not or could not support, lived in the midst of desperate measures. How, women religious wanted to know, can you minister to women and do nothing to ease this problem?

The world, to put it mildly, found itself seething with questions. And convents and monasteries were not free of them. At night they withdrew behind cloister doors to pray, perhaps. But during the day they were responsible for teaching the children of the world how to live Christian lives in the midst of it. How could that possibly be done if women religious were not part of it, not involved in it, not privy to its questions themselves?

The forces arrayed against the involvement of nuns in public events were mighty: in the early 1960s Bishop John Dearden of Pittsburgh, alarmed by the number of nuns who were going out to evening conferences or being seen with lay groups, encouraged laypeople to report to the chancery any sisters who were seen in public after 6:00 p.m. And they did. Three Benedictine sisters of Erie, returning from a long day's trip with student debaters, decided to eat in Pittsburgh after the forensic tournament rather than set out for Erie with nowhere to eat along the way. The local chancery got word of the sighting and a warning came from Bishop Dearden's office to the chancery in Erie the next day. Yet the silent revolution went on.

Society hovered on the edge of upheaval. But nonprofessed religious — candidates, novices, and scholastics — were not permitted either to be involved in its various dimensions or even to read newspapers. We rushed to wrap the kitchen garbage in order to get a glimpse of last week's headlines. To this day, people talk about the Korean War as the war they "missed."

Television sets never became common in the monastery till, after the election of John F. Kennedy in 1960, sets brought in by special permission so that history teachers could follow the proceedings simply never went out again.

The whole myth of being able to function in this world professionally and withdraw from it at the same time began to crumble. Jesus, people began to remember, was in the words of scripture "in the world but not of it." That was the problem. That was the emerging spiritual question: How were religious to be "in the world" but not "of it" at a time when the questions simply would not go away and the answers grew more and more uncertain every day?

It is in this social climate, both inside religious life as we lived it then and outside the church, that John XXIII called the first ecumenical council of the church in almost seventy-five years.

10

The New Theology

AN INTERNAL AGENDA

WOMEN RELIGIOUS, once the children of the church, took the Vatican documents seriously. In 1962, for the first time in four hundred years, the bishops of the church, gathered in an ecumenical council, looked at the world around them and the role of the church in its midst. It was not the world addressed by the Council of Trent in 1545, whose reaction to the Protestant Reformation had simply been to defend all past positions and to introduce even more rigid controls. Nor was it the world in which Vatican I, surrounded by the dry bones of fallen monarchies, had proclaimed papal infallibility in 1870.

The world of 1962 was a secularized, interconnected system of newly emerging democracies, communist totalitarian states, and "underdeveloped countries." All of them had been traumatized into change by almost seventy-five years of continual warfare. All of them were being held precariously together only by the fragments of a rapidly emerging global technology. All of them were, at the same time, being fractured by nuclear powers poised at the trigger points of their armed missiles. It was not a Catholic world, a theocratic world, a monarchial world, or a stable world. The church, on the other hand, embodied within itself a predisposition for all those earlier kinds of worlds and with them the danger of being seen in times such as this as hopelessly anachronistic.

The sixteen major documents that came out of Vatican II in response to such a social situation completely reframed both the role and the definition of church. The implications of them in a world such as this are with us still. The spiritual life was no longer business as usual. "Thank God," Christopher Fry wrote once, "that we live in an age when problems are soul-sized." It is a dangerous prayer. It demands that people fix their hearts on the spiritual fundaments of life rather than the spiritual trivia of life.

Women religious began to grow up over night. Unlike many in the church whose lives were touched by one or other of the positions in a particular way, the lives of religious were affected by every one of them. The way they looked at the church, the way they looked at the world and their role in it, the way they related to other people, both within the church and outside of it, were dictated by the philosophy, the theology, and the structural changes these documents brought with them.

Some groups, including bishops and priests, ignored the documents entirely. As the Irish tell it, for instance, when Archbishop John Charles McQuaid got off the plane from Rome, his first statement to the press made it clear: "Good people of Ireland," he said. "Do not fear. Nothing has changed." The story made the point. Whatever small cosmetic changes might be required of them, they would all go on as before, their vision unchanged, their minds unpersuaded.

Some groups resisted the documents and everything they implied. They withdrew into a psychological bastion inside Vatican I and set up camp. They brooked no transitions, tolerated no discussions, accepted no amount of change, and set out to intimidate or castigate anyone who did. The greater part of the church was blissfully unaware of any but the most obvious changes and got little of the theological explanations of them from the pulpit, in some cases because priests simply didn't care about the council, in many cases because they didn't understand the changes any better than many of their parishioners.

As a consequence, most of the church went on living a spiritual life that tottered on a continuum between confusion and chaos, doing the best they could to absorb the kiss of peace and the guitars that came with it in churches that once resounded with theater organs and caverns of silence. It was a tumultuous time.

Mary Margaret Kraus's term of office as prioress spanned the entire period. With the close of Vatican II, change had descended like a cataract on women religious. Most of those who knew Mary Margaret personally might surely have considered her an unlikely candidate for captain in times such as these. She was a gentle and loving woman, not made for conflict, it would seem. But it was exactly a leader like this who, perhaps, was best fitted to steer a small vessel through heavy water in the flotilla led by the Bark of Peter. Being prioress in the years between 1964 and 1978 was like standing on deck during a hurricane on the open sea. There was nowhere in sight that the storm wasn't raging.

There was nowhere where change wasn't buffeting the community in the person of at least one sister or the other. There was no community meeting at which at least one significant change wasn't ratified. All of them brought new public attention to the restructuring of religious life: there were changes in habit, changes in ministry, changes in lifestyle, changes in public participation. There was also no community meeting on change in which almost one-half of the community didn't deeply disagree with the other half. But in the midst of it all, there was no community decision she didn't honor during that time, regardless of the abuse she herself would have to take for it, either internally or publicly. Most of all, there was no sister she didn't support as the ship of community rocked and rolled. And they were everywhere doing everything that had never been done before.

Women religious across the country operated in every dimension of the church now. They worked in each and every type of parish, were subject to each and every type of bishop, dealt with each and every type of parent, struggled with each and every liturgist in the hope of making real what the Vatican documents made plain. But first of all, of course, they themselves had to come to grips with the meaning of each of the changes for their own community life.

They have been grappling with each of these questions every step of the way for over forty years now. Each of the documents represents a turning point in theological understanding so profound that, once recognized, the spiritual life can never be lived quite the same way again. Some were meant to recast the nature of the church itself; others to redefine the various "classes" of people within it. What it was to be the Catholic Church and what it was to be a Catholic in it gave new energy to an old church. It also gave that church new possibilities, new tensions — all of which touched women religious in deep and special ways.

The Church

In the Dogmatic Constitution on the Church (*Lumen Gentium*), for instance, the turning point is the very definition of the church itself. In pre–Vatican II Baltimore Catechism days, the definition of church was structural and straightforward. The church, every child learned, was "that body of the lawfully baptized who accepted the tenets of the faith, and were gathered around the local bishop who was in communion with the bishop of Rome." The image is a totally ecclesiastical one. Laypeople become the silent observers of a clerical church at work.

Vatican II enlarged that definition of church. The church, this council declared, is "the people of God." All the people of God. Here the focus shifts away from structures and authority, away from papacy and clericalism to the Christian community as a whole. The vision broadens beyond the hierarchical, beyond the image of lay consumers of a clerical product to a vision of people together in pilgrimage. But then the tensions multiply too.

The whole question of role definitions — of who does what, cleric or lay — becomes a major issue in parishes and diocesan offices everywhere. The place of intellectual giftedness and the responsibilities that attach to that become theological subject matter in church circles for the first time. Will final decisions be made by those professionally prepared to make them or will they be made by clerical authorities simply because they are clerics? Who is in charge of what and why become matters of serious contention in a church that purports to recognize the gifts of the laity as well as the position of pastor.

With the shift in the definition of church from clerical system to baptized community, relationships and ecclesiology — of who is more important than whom in the church and why — begins to become paramount for the first time in modern history. A narrowly educated clergy find themselves in a kind of theoretical standoff with a more broadly educated laity. The problem of who has the final say, those with the competence or those with a clerical collar, becomes a matter of major contention, a whole new point of theological departure.

As people, in other words, began to realize that they more than simply "belong" to the church but, in fact, are the church, whole segments of church society began to take that focus seriously. And in ways that altered past patterns and beliefs. They began to make clear that they want their church open to women, open to gays, open to married priests, open to women preachers, open to lay consultation. Open.

Not surprisingly, women religious who, at the time of the promulgation of documents such as these, occupied most of the nonclerical positions in the church — as administrators, principals, social service directors — found themselves deeply embroiled in the struggle to give lay authority real meaning in the church. In Erie, the sister supervisor of schools received an order from the priest superintendent of education to wear a veil in the office, "the sign of religious life," at all times. The determination of any type of official dress of the sisters, she decided, was a community matter, not a diocesan decision, and the community had long since determined that the veil was optional. The sister refused to go back to wearing it, despite the fact that she herself had never been in favor of abandoning one — and lost her job. The community needed the money and jobs were now not easy for nuns to come by with schools closing but Mary Margaret Kraus never flinched. The decision, she said, was Kathleen's.

Disputes with priests and pastors became commonplace, and the gulf between them that had commonly been there for other reasons now only widened.

Divine Revelation

The Dogmatic Constitution on Divine Revelation (*Dei Verbum*), on the place of scripture in Catholic formation, re-energized literary exegesis and historical scholarship. Fearful of a trend to "private interpretation of scripture," these areas of study had lain dormant in Roman circles for centuries until the document by Pius XII, *Divino Afflante Spiritu*, finally opened scripture to professional study in 1949 just in time to save the church from the equally serious question of scriptural literalism. At the same time, this fresh encouragement of biblical study raised other issues. The question of whether or not revelation is ongoing suddenly broke open the whole question of the development of both the faith and the church. Do the church and faith go on developing in every era, and if so how? Or has everything that can be said of the faith already been said, has all revelation ended, and if so what is to be done the next time a new Galileo appears to tell us that there is life on another planet? Then what must be said of the uniqueness of Jesus, for instance, or the nature of salvation, or the universal claims of a "tradition" that is clearly not universal?

The understanding of tradition began to broaden as well. As the Benedictine liturgist Godfrey Diekmann put it, "Tradition was not the stuff that was passed on; tradition was the passing on of the stuff." Tradition was the essential elements of the faith remembered but reembodied by every generation. An understanding of "tradition" that is based solely on historical patterns of practice and custom — the things we've "always done," like wear habits or have adoration of the Blessed Sacrament — rather than on the essential meanings of the faith, began to be contested at every level. Women religious resisted the static definition of "tradition" in favor of an understanding of tradition as ongoing commitment to gospel values, lived out differently from age to age. And with firm scriptural foundation. If scripture, for instance, has nothing at all to say about the ordination of women, on what basis do we use Jesus as our right to obstruct it? Is tradition nothing but the common cultural practices that have come down to us through time or is tradition those behaviors that are in accord with the essential demands of the gospel message? And if tradition is nothing but the accumulation of historical customs, then what of slavery, a practice condoned by the church for centuries?

The place of scripture in the development of doctrine — the model of Jesus more than the mandates of a time-bound church — took on new meaning for women religious. And with it usage after usage that could be argued to do more to obstruct the meaning of the gospel rather than to enable it dropped away. While bishops fumed from coast to coast at the sight of women religious on the streets rather than in parochial schools, women's communities opened drop-in centers and soup kitchens in the inner cities of the country in an attempt to follow the Jesus who had walked from Galilee to Jerusalem talking to tax collectors, prostitutes, and Roman soldiers, curing the sick and raising the dead.

In Erie, like the Jesus who fed the masses, Benedictine sisters opened a storefront soup kitchen for the poor and unemployed while people fumed that we were only encouraging indolence. Years later my own phone was still ringing with complaints about "the kinds of people" who were forming bread lines in front of the soup kitchen in downtown Erie. Mary Margaret braved the beginnings with a kind answer to each complaint but never so much as suggested that the sisters should think about closing the kitchen or turning the hungry away.

The Liturgy

Few of the documents of Vatican II had as immediate an effect on the church as the Constitution on the Sacred Liturgy (*Sancrosanctum Concilium*). With its institution of the vernacular, in this case English, as an "official" language of consecration, the liturgy of the church became the property of the people. For the first time in centuries, congregations understood the words of consecration, the texts of scripture, the hymnody of the Mass. The use of strange language, mesmerizing as it might have been, transcendent as it might seem, nevertheless gave "the holy mysteries" more "mystery" than meaning. Now people found themselves confronted with the call of the Eucharist as the leaven of life, not an escape from life.

Gone was the notion that Eucharist was something done for us and on us instead of with us. The celebration of Eucharist as something for a single priest in a dark crypt to "get in" so the world could be "saved" became, almost overnight, an act of Christian community by a people in search, a people in the process of conversion.

It was all a great breakthrough for the theology of Christian community.

But tensions lurked in those shadows too. Uniformity, that long-heralded counterpoint of Catholic unity, became a point of contention that surfaced nowhere more quickly than it did in convents and monasteries of women. In one community after another, one group adhered to the notion of Eucharist as a kind of immersion in the mystical while other members of the same congregation read the new eucharistic theology as a commitment to become immersed in the cries of humankind.

The liturgy became a battleground where bread recipes as well as the gender, dress, and geography of ministers around the altar threatened to alienate as much as unite. Mystique became confused with mystery. Religious communities began to schedule separate liturgies rather than common liturgies. Some of the celebrations were for traditionalists and stayed comfortably quiet and securely routine. Some were for those for whom English hymns now meant more than polyphony or chant. As women became more and more aware of their marginalization in church and society, the Eucharist itself became a particularly painful daily reminder of it. Eucharist, meant to be the glue that held a religious community together, the very reason for the life, became suddenly a symbol of what most divided them. In Erie, for instance, a group of jubilarians decided that as much as they would like to have their priest friends attend the Mass of celebration, they did not think that concelebration was appropriate in this situation. This jubilee Mass, after all, was a celebration of the lives of the sisters, not a celebration of the priesthood.

Mary Margaret inserted a card in the community invitation to clergy invitees explaining the community decision to forego concelebration and telling priests that there was no reason, therefore, for them to bring their vestments to the celebration. As a result, some priests refused to come to the Mass at all.

As women religious became more and more conscious of their invisibility in the church, attendance at liturgies became for them, as for their lay sisters, more the problem than the solution to the renewal of the church.

The Church in the Modern World

From an insular perspective that emphasized the separateness of the sacred and the secular, the church in the Pastoral Constitution on the Church in the Modern World (*Gaudium et Spes*) turned squarely to the consideration of the integrity and the essential connectedness of the sacred and the secular.

It was a transfiguring moment.

From a posture of parochial resistance and rejection of the larger world, the church suddenly became a voice on the side of human advancement, the development of world community, the acceptance of science, and a new concern for the economic and cultural development of all peoples as well as for their spiritual salvation.

The transformation of society, in other words, rather than simply the transformation of the self, is publicly declared in this keystone document to be an essential part of the church's mission to humanity.

In these things religious became consciously and clearly embroiled. Women's communities, in large part, had concern for the poor at the very roots of their congregations. And it was to the needs of the poor to whom they wished, almost intuitively, to return. And so the tensions emerging out of this document became disturbingly clear. Whose side were religious supposed to be on? The side of the poor, many of whom were not Catholic and most of whom sought the kind of help that was outside the historical boundaries of the church, or on the side of the institutions that had educated an entire population, once immigrant and now, ironically, a large part of the Establishment itself, whose policies were increasingly inimical to the development of the poor?

The question of how much involvement is too much involvement of church and professional church people in the political system and political issues lurked at the edges of every ministry decision. When does advocacy become improper for religious? When we argue for moral principles in the marketplace, whose morality shall it be and who decides? And how? Does work with or for the poor imply endorsing candidates, condemning candidates, forbidding the support of a candidate to people, to adults, to citizens of conscience — or teaching principles?

In Erie, sisters joined the black community to resist segregation. Then sisters became involved in the peace movement and demonstrations against the war in Vietnam. When Jane Fonda came to town, Pax Center, a group of Erie Benedictines, sponsored the event. The outcry was shrill and long. For years, the civic community of this small town reacted angrily about it. Was this treason or was this Christianity? Should sisters be doing such things? What did we have to do with such things anyway? Our role, we had always been told, was to obey the government.

Women religious found themselves in strange territory, indeed. The consequences of moving out of historical ministries in Catholic schools, hospitals, and care homes to serve a larger population in nonsectarian ways bewildered the Catholic population whose children were left without teaching sisters and disquieted those whose understanding of religious life included seclusion and denominational identity.

The Episcopal Office

In the Decree on the Bishops' Pastoral Office in the Church (*Christus Dominus*), the council made a screeching turn in the episcopal ministry from medieval potentate to modern pastor. The bishop, consequently, is not defined in these documents as lord and lawgiver. His role is said to be to enable the church, to be in touch with issues and ideas, to create a national identity.

Nevertheless, the question of international control of the newly heightened local church is the high water still being negotiated now. Unless the tension between Roman control and national identity is resolved, pastoral paralysis — the inability of the local church to implement the documents of Vatican II in ways that are proper to that church at that time — will surely set in with a vengeance. Ecclesiastical climbing for official favor will surely take over as bishops defer to Roman control rather than stand for national needs. Then, in the end, bishops will easily become unnecessary at all.

To fly in the face, for instance, of national conferences of bishops and their authorization of liturgical translations for their own countries not only obviates the local church but makes a local bishop purely ornamental as well.

Women religious, formed to build up the local level of the church everywhere, took local implementation of the documents of Vatican II seriously. They pressed for changes on the local level and found themselves repeatedly in conflict with local bishops — over the unremitting use of male language, over jurisdiction, over community renewal programs. In some cases, the bishop was himself uncommitted to the council. In later years, bishops felt powerless to change things for fear of being corrected for it by officials at the Vatican.

It was an uneasy time for both bishops and religious. In Erie, sisters moved out of the monastery to live in an old frame house in a poor neighborhood, much as they had when the community first came to Erie over 125 years before. "Apartment living," the bishop called it ruefully, as if living in a real house relating to real people was not at least as much a witness as living in a palatial house miles away from anybody at all.

But the issue was bigger than the type or size of house. The issue was that bishops could no longer depend on diocesan religious to do their bidding and women religious could no longer depend on bishops to affirm their work. The cleavage in what had been tightly knit diocesan systems became obvious. And difficult.

Priesthood and Priestly Formation

The Decree on the Ministry and Life of Priests (*Presbytero-rum Ordinis*) and the Decree on Priestly Formation (*Optatam Totius*) may someday be seen as pivotal to the development of the new church to which the earlier documents point. In these documents clericalism died an official death — however prevalent it remained on the ground.

What is asked of the priest in these documents is the ability to form community, to lead the search for God, but to acknowledge, to listen to, and to trust the laity whose gifts, the same documents say, are essential to the church.

As the document's telling phrase "brother among brothers" (*sic*) celebrates,[4] the priest is to be spiritual catalyst, not parish CEO. But the role revision sounds a great deal easier in theory than it came to be in practice. "Father says" in a church where "the people of God" come to know themselves as the church is no longer enough to qualify unilaterally for the running of a school, a ministry, or a parish. Laypeople are beginning to

demand accountability. Worse, laypeople are often better educated to administer the very projects turned over to clerics
simply because they are clerics.

In these documents, however, from a position of "Father" —
the patriarchal lawgiver of a Roman family in whose hands lay
the life or death of the entire clan — the priest is now asked
to assume the role of "brother," of caring peer, of loving equal,
even to the married and to women. The change in terms, a not
insignificant transition if the church is ever to truly be church
rather than simply a clerical establishment with laws to prove
it, reimagines the entire structure of the church.

Women religious began to find themselves in administrative roles in parishes, church ministries, and even chanceries.
But then the problems really arose: Who was the pastor, Sister or Father? And if not this one or that one, why not? And
if Sister, is she the final word or only the public word? Is the
authority real or fictional? And on what grounds is authority
in the church dispensed? On grounds of baptism or only of
ordination? In which case, are laypeople only staff to priests,
not really people with "the rights and duty" to give their gifts
to the church which the canons describe?

In Erie, a clash of authority between the principal of the
school and the pastor of the parish over an administrative matter in the school led to the sister's resignation from what had
long been an honored position for her. The pastor wanted to
placate the parents; the sister wanted to maintain the standards of the school. She was a professional educator; he had
never taught a day in his life. She may well have been wrong.
But no one will ever know for sure. There was no court of appeal. The pastor, much like a feudal lord, reigned as the last
word in the every parish.

Clearly, the documents of Vatican II provided a cornucopia
of possibility, a labyrinth of change. For women religious, both
the private embodiment of a distinct kind of Christian life and
one of the clearest symbols of public change, the years were a
minefield of new meanings and new misunderstandings in the
church.

For women who had been totally absorbed in carrying to a new generation the very meaning of the life of the church — its definition, its liturgy, its authority structures, and its role — these documents completely reordered their lives in the church.

But there were social and personal changes as well.

11

The New Theology

THE EXTERNAL AGENDA

VATICAN II, women religious came to realize, was about a great deal more than simply the renewal of the internal structures of the church or a theological study of its basic nature. The episcopacy, priesthood, revelation, liturgy, and self-definition — all issues of the institutional self-concept of the church — had impact, of course. These topics, however, were not the issues that changed the public presence or image of the church. The documents of Vatican II that deal with questions of relationships among the people of God and with the rest of humankind loomed equally as large. In fact, in the long run these other issues may be seen as the most meaningful of all, at least to the functioning of the church in the public arena.

The world's perception of the church at the time of Vatican II made it wary of all things "Catholic." Seen to be largely insular, forbidding, unyielding in its rigidity, and unrelenting in its claim to absolute truth, Catholicism was declining in Europe and existing as a subculture in the United States. The function of the church revolved around the conversion of the rest of the world to Catholicism, not simply as a participant in its sanctification.

More menacing than the drive to proselytizing, however, was the practice of the church to reject en masse the spiritual value of the rest of humankind. What was not Catholic, in those days, was not acceptable, was not holy.

Mixed marriages — marriage between a Catholic and a Protestant — were somehow wrong, even if they were "right," meaning saved from total opprobrium by the promise to raise all the children Catholic.

Children were taught that to go into a Protestant church was to commit a mortal sin. As the only Catholic in my stepfather's Presbyterian family, I went to Sunday school with my Protestant cousins during family vacations and, just as regularly, confessed it. The fact that I had learned about Moses and Samson and the birth of Jesus from Protestant teachers made something suspect about the situation. Everything they said sounded right enough to me but it was Protestant and therefore wrong. All wrong.

But if Protestants were bad, Jews were traitors and everybody else — Buddhists and Hindus and Muslims — were pagan.

It was a world of insiders and outsiders. Us and them. Our side and their side. Right and wrong. And we were the ones who were right.

Nuns, in particular, were a special part of this system. After all, they were the ones who taught the rules to children that kept the divisions real. Nuns modeled the exclusion of a sinful world, meaning any world that was not entirely "Catholic." They symbolized the withdrawal, the separateness. They signaled the implacable unchangeability of the church. But however much an older generation took security and refuge in that physical demonstration of our "otherness" or the "discipline" of the church, the younger generation of Catholics had already begun to reject it.

The year Vatican II opened in 1962, drive-by carloads of students lit the fuse on "Molotov cocktails" — milk bottles full of gas — and threw them on the porch of a local convent. No one doubted for a moment that the teenage students who threw them were Catholics. Protestants would not have bothered, but Catholic students were already alienated from nuns, were angry at nuns, who were nameless symbols of a rigid system.

Perhaps no other changes in the church affected nuns as much as did the documents on the relationship of the church to the rest of humankind.

The Role of the Laity

That the role of the laity in the church was even an issue at Vatican II may be the greatest turning point of the church's modern history. In the Decree on the Apostolate of the Laity (*Apostolicam Actuositatem*), the lay state in the church began, for the first time in history in an official document of the church, to be described as a "vocation" and treated theologically. What's more, the laity are instructed in this document to realize that believers "have both a right and a duty to use their gifts" in the church. But if that is the case, participation rather than passivity becomes a major factor of lay commitment.

From that rationale came the call to the laity to be responsible for church organization, for Catholic education, for religious formation programs, for church administration, for thoughtful reflection — for the *sensus fidelium* — that John Henry Newman gifted to the modern church.

The document opened the floodgates of a church-in-waiting. Laypeople flocked to the pastoral ministry and church administration programs that qualified them to do it. They got degrees in theology. They studied canon law. They moved into Catholic schools in overwhelming numbers. But it wasn't all as easy in practice as it looked on paper. The operational assumption seemed to be that lay personnel would come into the ministry as low-paid volunteers or parish aides. Lay ministers had something completely different in mind.

The inherent tension in this development of the laity showed itself quickly. The problems were at least twofold. First, the departure from clericalism raised the issue of authority. When the competency required of the position lies with the lay leader, people wanted to know, to what degree is the priest in charge of parish administration or the school, for instance, and why?

In the second place, if the laity really are gifted for the sake of the Christian community, does this mean lay women, too, or only lay men?. And if it does mean women why are they not being accepted in worship or administration, into the diaconate at least, for which there are centuries of women deacons as models? On this issue in particular, history, theology, and law all came together to confront and expose the debilitating sexism of the church.

Ironically, bishops and priests became wary of the very lay ministers whose commitment could assure the ongoing development of the church at a time when few were entering seminaries and convents and the median age of nuns and priests was rising rapidly. Instead, many closed lay ministry programs, refused to hire laypeople, or terminated parish projects altogether rather than turn them over to lay administration. Laywomen, in particular, many of them nuns, were presenting themselves to bishops everywhere wanting to minister in the church — begging to minister in the church. In Erie, Mary Margaret gave permission for a sister to matriculate for a master's of divinity degree at a major seminary in the United States with the male candidates for the priesthood there. But when she returned, degree in hand, the diocese preferred to reassign a retired priest, whose energies were too low for much more than daily Mass, to be pastor of a church rather than accept the sister with a divinity degree who applied to be pastoral administrator. Instead of being welcomed, women everywhere soon discovered that, council documents or no council documents, their services were not being sought.

The results were farther reaching than anyone might have imagined. Rather than simply accept the fact that church ministry was not the option they expected it to be, many women went to Protestant seminaries for theological and pastoral preparation and stayed there to be ordained. Others, nuns especially, began their own spirituality programs, retreat centers, or women's groups. Faith-sharing groups, scripture study centers, and spiritual direction programs sprang up everywhere. Catholic schools became almost entirely lay-led while nuns branched out into interdenominational work or private programs. More than that, the likelihood that nuns and laywomen would participate together, on equal footing, as partners and collaborators in ministry, only increased. Distinctions were eroded, divisions were erased.

Suddenly, the work of the church began to be done outside the boundaries of the institutional church itself. The "people of God" had begun to take themselves seriously. Where renewal programs failed to be a diocesan priority, the people created their own. But the problem remains.

If Roman Catholic dioceses continue to refuse to prepare women for participation in the church, this movement of Catholic women to Protestant schools of theology will significantly alter the shape of the church in the next twenty-five years. It is the very preparation of the laity that guarantees the church as institution as well as the passing on of the faith.

Ecumenism

The wide divide common to the Catholic and Protestant communities, a legacy of Europe's long wars of religion and the division of national territories on religious grounds that followed them, finally ended at Vatican II. The Decree on Ecumenism (*Unitatis Redintegratio*) gave official recognition to the scandal of Christian division. What is more, the statement asserted a unity in vision and essential commitment common to the whole Christian family. It gathered in, under one umbrella for the first time in four hundred years, those followers of Christ who were not Roman Catholic but were definitely Christian nevertheless.

With the recognition of the common ground that existed among all Christian churches, it made a distinction between the faith and the church. There were those who were Christian who were not Catholic. The discovery seems almost embarrassing in hindsight, but for the people of the time, it was cataclysmic. Whole families had been split over the ecclesiastical standoffs that were part and parcel of the Reformation.

Catholics were forbidden to attend the marriages, even of their own children, to Protestants. Protestants were taught that Catholicism was a foreign-dominated (Roman) religion that threatened the very existence of democracy. National elections were won and lost on the religious issue in a country that prided itself on its "separation of church and state."

Vatican II changed all of that. The Catholic Church stepped across the line and opened its arms to its "separated brethren" and, almost overnight, the religious climate of the United States changed. The document on ecumenism affirmed the diversity of gifts — liturgical, spiritual, and theological — that make up the whole church of Christ in all its denominations. War waged in the name of Christ for centuries was, it seemed, over. But then, for that reason alone, a new struggle began.

The challenge to move ecumenism beyond the realm of ecclesiastical get-togethers, to the recognition of the single mission and the common table of the total Christian church became both major — and problematic — at the same time.

Women religious, more than the rest of the church, or at least in more formal ways, imaged the divisions that grew up between the Reformers and the Vatican in the sixteenth century over "the theology of the higher vocation." In their zeal for "the priesthood of all believers," Protestant Reformers as a group had discounted and eliminated the whole concept of religious life. With the document on ecumenism, the questions of independence from papal control, the charism of the churches, and the nature of religious life itself emerged all over again. But this time on a different scale and out of different mind-set. The problem now was the hard task of reconciliation and the genuine acceptance of the differences inherent in each tradition. Women religious began to perform an important, though unofficial, role in the process.

Once women religious realized that the common Christian role in mission could and must be shared, they began to join ranks with Christian ministers everywhere. When they began to realize that the theological distinctions that constituted the Catholic-Protestant gulf were, after the council's restatement of Christian dogma, more fictional than real, they began to join ecumenical prayer groups and ecumenical social movements and find new spiritual energy there. When they began to see not only what could be respected in other traditions but must be respected, they began to read the great Protestant theologians in order to bring depth to their own ecumenical conversations. Most of all they became key participants in bringing honor and legitimacy to the ecumenical movement on local levels. They attended Protestant conferences, wrote for Protestant journals, participated in Protestant liturgies, and drew personal strength from their Protestant associations.

In Erie, Mary Margaret opened the chapel to the Lutheran community and joined with the community in the common prayer service. This very simple act of genuine Benedictine hospitality built a bridge to the local Protestant community that grew stronger by the year.

Eventually, as a result of the spiritual intensity that kind of personal association and formal interaction produced, the struggle between being Christian and being Catholic began to show itself. Once prime members of the Catholic ghetto, women religious launched out into the larger Christian world, working with Protestant ministers, leading ecumenical projects, sharing prayer and liturgies, studying in both Protestant and public schools of higher learning.

The world got bigger for women religious and its demands on them grew. Having distinctly "Catholic" institutions, doing distinctly "Catholic" teaching faded in importance. The waters began to merge and at the same time the lifelong need to be a "good Catholic" found itself superseded by the need to be a good Christian. Now even the church itself could be evaluated on those terms. It was a moment of shocking theological maturity.

It became clear that the scandal of division is not the scandal of the people. It is the scandal of the professional church makers who taught it. And, religious came to understand, it must be repented before we can begin to teach the peace of Christ to anyone else.

The difference between indifferentism and ecumenism had lost its edge. Instead, the absolutism that erodes the witness of the full Christian presence — even when it came packaged in later documents from Rome — failed to persuade.

Religious began to realize that conversion and repentance are imperatives of the church as well as of its members.

Missionary Activity

The turning point in the Decree on the Church's Missionary Activity (*Ad Gentes*) is attitudinally so deep that perhaps only a Catholic can sense its real depth. Two new postures are affirmed here. The first is that conversion must be free. With this statement hundreds of years of church-state control are abandoned by a church whose entire middle history was embedded in theocratic governments. The very idea that religion can be tied to statehood — or statehood to religion — lost all coinage.

The missionary life, once geared to the conversion of whole peoples, had, with this council document, suddenly become an exercise in personal spiritual growth and Christian witness. Like Charles de Foucauld, founder of the Little Brothers and Sisters, whose only "missionary" activity was to live a Christian life in a Moslem village, the missiology of Vatican II called missionaries to be deponents of the Christian life, not sellers of Christian politics.

The second notion is that missionaries are, in the too lately discovered spirit of the Jesuit missionary Matteo Ricci, to be more presence than proselytes. They are to become inculturated and, as quickly as possible, enable the new church to become native. The purpose of missionary activity is not simply to convert people to a Western form of Catholicism. It is to allow the culture to flourish in a native church.

According to the document, Western ecclesiastical imperialism is over. However, the growing shift in the center of the church from global North to global South in population, character, and tone did little or nothing to dislodge Roman curial control. Tension is inherent here.

How long new native churches will tolerate Western formulations, interpretations, liturgical forms, and theology is anybody's guess. The Chinese church, the Asian church, and that other newly recognized mission church — the American one — have begun to become themselves. It is a dangerous moment, not for the local church but for Rome.

The turning point in this document on the relationship of the church to non-Christian religions had as much impact in the Christian West as it did in other parts of the non-Christian world. It was a time bomb waiting to go off. In a dramatic move, this declaration from a council of the church solemnly assembled asserts that as Christians we must accept "all that is true and holy" in non-Christian religions. In Buddhism, in Hinduism, in Judaism. In Islam.

After centuries of their repudiation, moreover, the church officially condemned in this statement any persecution or discrimination based on race, color, condition of life, or religion. The implications for world development and the creation of human community were far-ranging. But they were nowhere more far-ranging than in the convents and monasteries of the West. Zen Buddhism, Sufi myths, and Jewish Kabbalah made common cause with Christian mysticism. Hindu flower and fire devotions and Zen koans became the stuff of Christian metaphor and ritual. When the sisters, for instance, introduced dance and drama into liturgy the priest-chaplain reported the community to the bishop. But Mary Margaret, documents in hand, held out, and dance went on in the chapel when it didn't exist anywhere else in the city.

The translation of the faith into the language and images and assumptions of other cultures became both a challenge and a pitfall. It opened the eyes of the people of the church to other kinds of imperialism, other kinds of differences as well. Discrimination based on sexual orientation became suspect, even when practiced by the church itself. The consideration of women as still outside the pale of God's agency became unacceptable. Differences lost credence as ground for any kind of discrimination anywhere under any circumstances.

Women religious, with their contact with young people and immigrants, interfaith work and academic life, were in the center of the spiritual and cultural storm. In Erie, Mary Margaret supported the opening of an ecumenical mission in Mexico, not simply to convert people, but to live and work among the people of a largely isolated area in the hope of helping them develop and direct the services they needed there. With declining numbers of religious in Erie itself, the move was a brave one. Why allow people to go "there" when sisters were needed here? Why allow a sister to be so far away from "the community," meaning outside of Erie? For Mary Margaret, the reasons were plain: these were people with a special need; this was a sister with a special gift; this was a community whose own spiritual growth would be extended by this new consciousness of the unlike other.

Eventually, the sister who started the mission decided to commit herself entirely to that work for the rest of her life. She withdrew from official religious life in the Erie Benedictines to immerse herself totally in the Mexican church and society. But Mary Margaret and Erie went on supporting the group regardless. The whole notion of church, of community, of mission had broadened far beyond the old notion of local work and "community" projects.

The implications of this seeping of spiritual boundaries went deeper than anyone ever expected. The effects of pluralism on governments and politics in this new multicultural world taxed the notion of personal freedoms and civil rights across the world. Would the Ten Commandments be enshrined in a U.S. courthouse? Would head scarves be allowed to Muslims in Western schools? Could liturgies be constructed out of the symbols of other peoples and other religions? Should prayer in schools and public support for private schools be supported or not? And if so, what kind of prayer and what beliefs should be supported? Were the Judeo-Christian commandments really the basis of Western jurisprudence? And when is pluralism too much pluralism? When does pluralism threaten the very pluralism that as a nation we espouse and as a global people we can no longer avoid.

Women religious learned quickly that it was no longer necessary to learn to function in a non-Christian world that was essential to Christian ministry. It was learning to function as Christian in a non-Christian neighborhood, which, it became clear, was essential to both world and church. When what once were Catholic schools and Catholic soup kitchens and Catholic social service centers now serve a population that is no longer Catholic — no longer Christian — either in culture or in tradition, the Declaration on the Relationship of the Church to Non-Christian Religious (*Nostra Aetate*) and the way we relate to non-Christian religions comes instantly into play.

Religious Freedom

In the Declaration on Religious Freedom (*Dignitatis Humanae*) the revolutionary tenet is simply that conscience must be the primary determinant of religious conviction. Everyone — everyone — the church says, even nuns and priests, apparently, is immune from coercion in the name of religion. The problem is clear: someone, somewhere must come to grips with coercion. Is the attempt to suppress Christian ministers from raising questions of faith "coercion"? Is legislative pressure to write morality into law "coercion"? And, if it isn't, whose morality shall it be in a multicultural society, in a world without borders? What is the line between church and state? Between church and conscience? What is the place of questions in individual faith development and what does that have to do with the development of doctrine? The answers are not simple ones but, many a nun or priest has discovered since Vatican II, you can't have spiritual freedom in one category but not in another.

In Erie, sisters did prayer services for peace on the steps of the cathedral at a time when most people supported the Vietnam War. Parents took students out of the community

academy in protest of the community's lack of patriotism. En-
rollment declined and with it the financial base of the school.
But Mary Margaret, always kind, always strong, stood firm.
Better that the academy should go than that the community
should ignore the gospel.

Religious Life

Over four hundred years after the Council of Trent thought
it had cast religious life in stone by declaring solemnly that it
was just right as it was — no more ministries to consider, no
more forms to create, no new orders to allow, no new rules to
permit beyond those of the early orders — the Second Vatican
Council called religious life to renew itself.

More importantly, perhaps, in the Decree on the Appropriate Renewal of the Religious Life (*Perfectae Caritatis*) the
council instructed religious to turn to the gospels, the initiating
intent of their founders, and the social realities of the times —
not to church law or episcopal control — for their criteria and
direction.

And these are all dangerous directions.

The concerns surfaced almost immediately and are with us
still. The dualistic notion that the essence of religious perfection lies in separation from the world lingers pathologically
in the minds of a generation formed on false or symbolic asceticisms rather than on the searing demands of a gospel that
cures lepers, raises women from the dead, and contends with
scribes and Pharisees. Transcending the world, then, becomes
a counterweight to transforming it. Consequently, the renewal
of religious life becomes a struggle to balance the claims of law
against the touchstone of an experience rife with new poor,
alive with new questions, challenged by new kinds of spirituality — new kinds of spiritual adults — and swirling from the
agenda of Vatican II itself.

Of the ministries listed in the Kennedy Directory, the reg-
istry of official Catholic organizations in the United States,
over 75 percent were founded by religious communities while

they were being scolded for leaving the schools and not wearing uniforms.

Finally, the question of whether or not religious life is to be fundamentally prophetic, as the Vatican documents said, or functionally institutional simmers at the center of the renewal of religious life. Are religious to animate or are they simply to staff the works they undertake in a church in which all are called to minister and lead and teach and serve? The issue may well be a determining one for the vitality of religious life in the future.

Are women religious to be "the good sisters," the darling daughters of the church, or must they be dangerous women sent from the tomb with a message on their minds? And a gospel in their hands?

It will be years, perhaps, before it's clear how many rivulets it will take to form the river of religious renewal. It may take even longer to assess which runnel will run strongest. But the struggle between canonical propriety and the demands of charism erupted early on in the renewal period and continues getting clearer every day.

Part Three

Development

It wasn't difficult to recognize the things in religious life that no longer had real spiritual value. Speaking fault about losing pins and spilling water, for instance, simply had no meaning to women who were operating schools whose budgets ran into the hundreds of thousands of dollars. Kneeling down to ask for soap and deodorant, once extravagant and unusual expenditures perhaps but now trifles, and necessary trifles at that, only annoyed a woman when it did not amuse her. Those elements of the life women put down easily — and with relief. What took the place of those symbols of self-abnegation, a popular spiritual word from an earlier period, was the asceticism of distinguishing healthy asceticisms from unhealthy asceticisms.

One age of religious life was dimming; a new age beckoned in the distance. But what was it? What did it look like? The giddy relief of seeing tired and now pointless practices disappear obscured another reality entirely: with the arguably banal but long sacralized dimensions of the life banished, what was left of it? It was a time of transition, of course, but to what?

Simply dismantling the assumptions of a past era, we soon learned, had little or nothing to do with making a successful bridge to a new one.

In the first place, new eras evolve slowly. They do not appear overnight. Scripture is clear about it: the chosen people

wandered for forty years in the desert "until the older genera-
tion died off." Social transition demands that people be given
the opportunity not simply to put down old ideas but to try out
some new ones along the way.

In the second place, people must be ministered to tenderly
in times of great change. None of us is independent of the ideas
that formed us. They tell us what our world is like. They tell us
our proper place in it. They tell us who we are. To lose those
definitions is to lose the very mainstays of our lives. To lose all
of them at once is even more traumatic.

Development of ideas and the development of people go
hand and hand, then. All the time we are exploring new ways
to go about life, it is equally important that we support in their
personal growth the people who will be most affected both by
the loss of the past and the demands of the new future. After
all, however irrelevant the things of the past may now be, they
are at least familiar. However enticing the future may seem, it
is at best unpredictable.

The problem is that in times of great change, it is the past
that is clear and the future that is formless. Uncertainty sets
in and, for many people, fear with it. The loss of the familiar
leads to a lack of self-confidence for some. The bravado com-
mon to many, the excitement characteristic of some at the
thought of the newness that drives change, gives way com-
monly to disillusionment, to depression, to anomie or a sense
of purposelessness so deep that the very institution itself is in
danger of simply disappearing. Women who were most will-
ing to stop wearing medieval clothing suddenly discovered that
they did not now know what to wear at all. Sisters who were
most eager to have flexibility in the schedule began to wonder
why, with the loss of the herd mentality, there was any reason
to stay in religious life at all. Sisters who had long wanted to
be able to make their own decisions about time and work and
living situations found themselves unwilling to move now for
fear there would be nowhere to go, nothing to do in the future.

Now it was not so much what was happening that mat-
tered, it was the people to whom it was happening that

became the subject matter of renewal. Now whole generations of faithful religious found themselves without mooring, without direction, without a clear understanding of the life and themselves in it.

The task of such a period is support for new possibilities, yes, but it is also about the development of confidence and creativity among the peoples themselves. These are peoples of the desert and the promised land is a long way off.

12

The Cutting Edge of Change

W HETHER THE RENEWAL PERIOD of religious life signals a period of genuine change in both religious life and the church or simply a series of aborted adjustments masking as renewal is yet to be seen. Whatever the final outcome, no one doubts that it was a period of profound struggle between the force of change and the forces of reaction. The impulse to follow the gospel and the council documents to their inevitable conclusions found itself at odds with the need to move in harmony with a church that too often did not want to move at all, all documents to the contrary.

The psychological reality of change is that it is always entrusted to the generation most likely to be adversely affected by its coming. Elting Morison, whose studies of innovation became classics in the social psychology of change, cites the famous example of the British defense of the English coast toward the end of the World War II. Pushed back against their own cities, the English faced the possibility that they would be overrun by Hitler's army. There was no doubt that this last stand could end in veritable extinction of the nation. With their supplies and armaments lower than they had ever been, they returned to the use of the horse-drawn canons left over from the First World War. To give them mobility on the coastline, they attached the old guns to the back of trucks, this time in order to be able to move them more quickly from position to position than could the horses for which the initial carriages had been designed. However mobile the units, though, the gunners themselves were slow. The army called for a time-motion study of the action.

Everything about the use of the new gunnery defenses seemed smooth, with one exception. Just before firing, two members of the five-man team halted all activity, snapped to attention and stood there for three full seconds during the duration of the firing. They hoisted no shells, readied no fuses, took no loading positions. They just stood there taut and at attention by the back of the gun.

No one could account for such a strange response under fire and at the height of attack. Finally, they called in a retired colonel to study photographs of the routine. What, the researchers asked the colonel, was the purpose of that kind of motion? For a moment even the colonel was puzzled. Then, he looked at the pictures again. "Aha," he said, "now I have it. They are holding the horses."[5]

The point is clear: when we are trained to respond in one way to one kind of situation, the transition to new ideas and new needs is long and slow, sometimes even resisted by the people who have both the most to gain from the fact of change, the most to lose from the breakdown of it. Gunners trained to steady the horses during the firing of the canons went on with the old routine even when there were no longer any horses to hold. The fact is that people commonly deal with change by continuing to respond in old ways, even to new circumstances, even when clinging to the familiar endangers the very security they seek.

The implications for the polarization arising out of an innate resistance to change both inside the community and among its traditional supporters consumed the administration of Mary Margaret Kraus. As the first prioress of the Benedictine Sisters of Erie to be called "sister" rather than "mother" — a telling move in itself — and "prioress" or "first among equals" rather than "superior," she herself symbolized the depth of the changes with which the community was dealing. The terminology itself indicated the distance from childhood to adulthood that religious life in general and the Erie Benedictines in particular had managed to travel in so short a time.

What the council fathers addressed in the documents of Vatican II looks innocuous now, perhaps, forty years later. Almost unimaginative, in fact. At the time of their writing, however, they were cataclysmic for those who were expected to implement or to live them. Mary Margaret Kraus's term of office is monument to both.

Change was in the air long before Mary Margaret became prioress of the Erie Benedictines in 1964. Vatican II had, after all, begun in 1962, a full two years before her election.

The church was geared for change. As the documents poured out of Rome, one after another, from one session of the council to the next, colleges, seminaries, theologians everywhere analyzed, predicted, and described the shifts in attitude and behavior that would be required if each of them were to become real.

The society, too, was geared for change. After almost half a century of war or threat of war, social tension, national sacrifice, and nuclear anxieties had reached a peak. Like steam escaping from a mountainside, newness was in the very air we breathed: the Beatles wrote a new kind of music; the country shifted to a new kind of urban life; suburbs erupted everywhere; mobility became the order of the day; teachers taught new ideas; computers and transatlantic hookups were on the horizon.

Finally, the community itself was geared for change. Schooled to adjust quickly during the administration of Alice Schierberl, however unorthodox the ideas, however unprepared for the project, the community, too, stood at the ready.

Alice had begun the deconstruction of the past. Mary Margaret would find herself completely engulfed by the need to concentrate on development in a world in transition. But no one knew exactly what that world was meant to look like. If there were limits that should be imposed on the changes, no one knew what they were. If there were dangers, no one could define them. If there was a way to stop it, no one knew how.

During the deconstruction period, Alice had been both leader and driver. In her time, monasteries revolved almost totally around the will of the superior. During the renewal period, Mary Margaret Kraus discovered what the researchers already knew: groups are as much responsible for what happens to a group as are their leaders. This one was chomping at the bit. Some wanted change; some feared it. Some wanted to go on driving change; some resisted being driven where they could not see to go. But one thing for sure: Mary Margaret was not a driver.

If there were two personalities that could correctly be described as polar opposites, they were Alice Schierberl and Mary Margaret Kraus. Alice was vivacious, excitable, assertive, and demanding. Mary Margaret was quiet, receptive, easygoing — and much stronger than anyone had ever guessed. Mary Margaret had been a first grade teacher all her life. She was patience personified. She had a way of disappearing into a group, even into a group she was leading. Those who didn't know her could be inclined to think that she wasn't leading at all.

The truth of the matter is that, unlike Alice, Mary Margaret did not press a group, she simply went her own way and let everyone else decide if they were going that same direction or not. The power of her simplicity, her total unwillingness to threaten anyone, made for a kind of changed environment that more required personal commitment than acquiescence. She was committed and she trusted that everyone else was as well. In Alice's community, you knew down deep that she might demand an explanation of your actions. In Mary Margaret's community, you knew just as deeply that you should be demanding of yourself an explanation of your actions.

The leadership style was endearing; it was also messy, without a sense of order, not rigid, not clear. It was an exercise in creativity rather than control. All the straight lines had broken down. Nor did she attempt to maintain them. Rather, she allowed all of us to move at our own speed, in our own way, on our own terms. It was a shock to the community mind. After all, when Alice had been prioress, Alice had been in charge. During Mary Margaret's administration, everyone on every end of the spectrum wondered if anyone was in charge. But unlike the situation in other groups where other superiors gave way to the tide of change without really engaging with it themselves, Mary Margaret left no doubt: she did not simply comply with renewal, she accepted the need for renewal and she embraced it herself. She had an almost unerring instinct for the gospel and a capacity to run with it lightfooted into the wind. Mary Margaret Kraus was leading by going there herself.

But the going took everything she had — all her physical energy, all her spiritual fortitude, every ounce of faith, every mite of courage.

One year after her election, Vatican II ended. Now the work of it fell to the chanceries, the churches, the seminaries, the parishes, the schools, the monasteries, and the convents of the world. Suddenly the euphoria of the council years broke down into the hard, bitter work of social change.

13

The Compass Points of Change

W HAT MARY MARGARET KRAUS inherited that Alice Schier-berl had not was an official mandate to change. *Perfectae Caritatis*, the Decree on the Appropriate Renewal of Religious Life, called every religious order in the world to renewal. Where Alice had had an instinct for renewal, the notion that something had gone mightily wrong in the way adult women were being asked to live religious life, Mary Margaret had the obligation to renew it according to what by now had become a slogan: "the vision of the founder, the needs of the members, and the signs of the times." Easier said than done.

The General Chapter of the federation to which the Erie Benedictines belonged determined early on in its proceedings that the charism of the Benedictine Sisters of the Federation of St. Scholastica was "to seek God in community and to respond in prayer and ministry" (Gen. Chap., 1974). There was nothing wrong with the ideas. On the contrary, the statement rang clear and true to the tradition. But its simplicity gave little hint of what would be its underlying complexity.

The compass points the charism statement defined to guide the group — community, prayer, ministry, and the lifelong search for God — were unarguable if all you were talking about were the niceties of history. After all, that's all Benedictines had ever done. There were no great defined tasks like converting the Indians, or building large hospitals for the poor, or educating African American children. Community building, regular choral prayer, simple ministries, and the search for God were the whole purpose, the real charism or gift of the life. But few among us, if any, realized at its beginning how far away and long the journey to its center might really be if you considered its social and psychological dimensions as well.

"Seeking God," the very hallmark of Benedictine life for almost fifteen hundred years, stood enshrined in the traditional prayer schedule of the community. It was neat. And it was impossible. An agricultural schedule developed in the sixth century, which had provided for over four hours a day in prayer and reading, had, over the years, been transplanted whole and entire to an urban, industrialized world of the twentieth century. No questions asked. That changed quickly, however. Now questions erupted everywhere.

The whole problem of how to "seek God" in a world ever more demanding of their presence and preparation became increasingly urgent. Sisters were not just tired; they were exhausted. The neatly organized schedule was beginning to tear apart at the seams. Nighttime and weekend activities — coaching the basketball team, attending parent-teacher meetings, directing school plays, holding choir rehearsals, traveling with the debate team, taking college courses — made every day longer and longer. But the schedule itself never changed.

The nature of the community Mass and prayer life began to be a major question. Was its very weight and length more a hindrance than a help in the seeking of God? Was it life-giving? Did it have anything whatsoever to do with life as it was lived here and now, in this century, in this place? With women? With real spiritual depth? Or was it simply part of the routine — and a barren one at that?

The concept of community life, rich and wonderful as it may sound, contained within it problems of its own. This element of the Benedictine tradition that distinguished it from "modern" orders formed more for the purpose of undertaking specified tasks — child care, teaching, nursing, evangelization — had become sterile. The rule of silence, meant to create a contemplative atmosphere, served to separate the community into a collection of isolated figures who could live together for years without ever really coming to know one another as people, as sisters. Even the spiritual experiences, gifts, and insights of other members went unknown and unnoticed. The task-orientation of the group had been honed to a fine point. The spiritual value of human relationships went almost completely unnoticed. We all lived alone together. Cheek by jowl.

Most sisters slept in large dormitories, some of them almost to the time they died, unless they lived in parish houses which, unlike the monastery in Erie, provided private rooms. There was no space, no time, no privacy, no sense of personal freedom. "I couldn't even find a place to cry," one young sister said just before she left the community. Young women entering religious life now were coming from a very different kind of world than the one that had engendered the one they discovered when they got there. Privacy, professional independence, freedom of movement, and a sense of personal responsibility — things uncommon, perhaps, to women of earlier centuries — were taken for granted by this one.

What's more, community-building, that characteristic of Benedictine life that had spawned whole villages of people around them in Europe, had been lost, at least for women, in the thirteenth century with the imposition of cloister. Now women lived a bifurcated life. They worked in the center of the people and avoided them entirely. Including their families. Few people came to the monastery; fewer still were invited into the center of it — even to pray with the community. Religious life had become a strange amalgam of public witness and personal retreat, a life within a life, a life unto itself. And that a relatively barren one, heavy on work, lacking in the kind of leisure that is truly reflective.

Finally, ministry had ceased to be a "response" to the desperate needs of an immigrant population and had begun to be more of an innocent burden. Sisters became teachers because that is all the community had ever done. And, besides, what else could be done? In most of the United States, sisters were not permitted to function outside the Catholic system, nor would they have been hired in a religious habit even if they had been permitted to try. In Pennsylvania, the Garb Act of 1894 even forbade religious in habits the right to enroll in day school courses in public universities in the United States. They were certainly not going to hire them.[6]

Instead, the community had only one ministry of its own, St. Benedict Academy, and that one competed for students with two other Catholic girls high schools in the area. Both of these other schools existed in more residential parts of town, attracted more professional clientele, and offered campus facilities that the inner-city Benedictines could not provide. By the time Mary Margaret Kraus became prioress in 1964, the ministry of the community had become a system of educational interchangeable parts designed to fill parish slots and expand the endlessly enlarging diocesan school system. The young woman who wanted to be a sister but did not want to be a teacher would have little interest in the Erie Benedictines. Either that or she risked dooming herself to a lifelong sense of dissatisfaction.

The idea of "seeking God, in community, and responding in prayer and ministry" had become a tangle of opposites, a contradiction in terms, a theological problem, a psychological paradox. It unleashed all the yearnings of the human soul.

At the same time, the hemorrhage of young women from the order had already begun. Between 1962 and 1982, 61 women entered the Erie Benedictine novitiate and 88 left. From 1962 through 1988, if professed members are included in the figure, 78 women entered and 101 left.

Something had derailed. Something had to be done. No one doubted that change was necessary but everyone, it seemed, defined it differently. Needing change and effecting change are two different things.

14

Obstacles to Change

HUMAN BEINGS do not change easily. Any administrator who tries to preside over periods of change can attest to the difficulty of the process. The fact is that the researchers are right: members have just as much power as any leader when they decide to use it. Resistance is built into every system, into most psyches, no matter how romantic our notions of the flexibility of any particular group, the oppression of any particular system, the desire of any group to be "liberated."

"Most men prefer to be slaves," Thomas Jefferson said once, long before there was any social scientific data to prove him right. I once taught in a new consolidated high school, for instance. In this particular school, seniors were originally dismissed out the center door, freshmen and sophomores left by the gym entrance, and juniors exited the building through the cafeteria. Two years later, when traffic patterns and class sites had been established, the headmaster changed the dismissal plan to have the seniors, whose afternoon classes were at the far end of the building, leave through the cafeteria door, rather than the center. No one on the faculty claimed later to have been prepared for the uproar that followed. The student body simply erupted in pain. We had violated the "traditions" of the school, student government representatives told us. We had never even asked them if it was all right, they said.

Maybe we should have realized right then and there that if you can't change an exit door for seventeen-year-olds for fear of destroying a tradition, or eliminate pumpkin pie from Thanksgiving dinner without the family disintegrating, to change an entire lifestyle would not be as easy as it may have seemed at first blush. No matter how sensible, how reasonable, how necessary the move, change in itself is traumatic. It shifts the expectations of people. It undermines their identity. It upsets their sense of security. It opens a Pandora's box of ambiguities and uncertainty.

But if there was anyone suited to attempt the process, it had to have been Mary Margaret. She went through life a saint of the relaxed grasp. Almost totally without ego, it seemed, she vested her own success in nothing but the understanding and acceptance of the people around her. She lived the rules herself, of course, and she taught them to the community. But she simply had no rigid or unyielding expectations of anyone. She was far more adept at explaining why sisters couldn't do a thing than why they must. The Rule of Benedict, monastic scholars taught repeatedly, was built on exceptions. If so, then it was Mary Margaret Kraus who most embodied the spirit of it.

She was slow to act, even slower to respond. Most significant of all, she was almost unerringly pleasant. Her emotional equilibrium hardly appeared to fluctuate from day to day. Her major physical problem, she said, was "low blood pressure." Her major emotional one, "the gift of tears," a kind of reflex reaction to pressures she felt but could never, or would never, articulate.

As the years went on and the pressures grew and her personality never broke under it, people began to joke that it was because she had low blood pressure — which she did — and simply couldn't get anxious or irritable. Low blood pressure, they joked, ought to be added to the chapter in the Rule on "The Qualities of the Abbot/Prioress." They would have been wrong, however. Mary Margaret suffered through renewal — and she suffered deeply.

She suffered with those for whom renewal was too fast. And she suffered even more for those for whom renewal was not fast enough. She suffered with the people who attacked her administration for being too lenient because she knew that they loved the life and wanted to be sure that it was lived well. She suffered with the people who were impatient with the temporizing because she knew their patience was almost at an end and that the loss of them would effect the energy of the community at large. In the course of a particularly bruising community meeting where over half the community voted to allow sisters to choose their own ministries rather than be appointed to them, she was even attacked because, in the mind of some, the majority vote was not as large a majority as they would have liked. In the course of the intermission, I found her leaning against a wall of a nearby room, her head in her hands, her eyes swollen. "Do you want to table this till the next time?" I said. "No," she said, her voice small but firm, "I want to get on with it."

She suffered — but she went relentlessly on.

Some might have called Mary Margaret a touch naive. After all, she trusted everyone. Those who knew her best, though, knew that what they were all seeing was faith. Simple, uncomplicated, unquestioned faith. Somehow God had gotten us into all of this, she knew, and somehow God would see us through it.

But the obstacles she faced in the process were overwhelming. They came without warning and they came without end. But they did not come without cause.

Monastic life, by its very nature and by virtue of its basic structures, is bound to be more conservative than most. Once the center of the rudderless agricultural culture of medieval Europe with its fallen governments and feuding societies, monasticism gave the society stability and direction. It was the religious orders that came later, however — the Franciscans, the Knights Templar, the Jesuits, the Salesians, the Vincentians — who plunged headlong into the social questions of a later age. By that time, Benedictines, burdened with the mixed blessing of having to look after rich farm land, moved less quickly. More than that, founded on a model that called for communal decision-making rather than a military model of centralized government, they moved more deliberately. At the same time, Benedictines, accustomed to working things through over long periods of time and as groups, expected to be consulted on community questions, not just told what to do. And consultation — when it's done well — takes time.

Where communities of Benedictine women were concerned, the rate of change was, at least until after Vatican II, by and large, even slower. Women as a class lacked the autonomy, self-confidence, and resources to undertake great institutional projects. Most of all, they had little or no freedom from male control even to try. Years of having to ask permission on their knees even to do what they were required to do kept them cautious, left them uncertain about what was good even for their own lives.

The thought of change in the way religious orders operated also met opposition from the publics that surrounded them. It was a time of foment and development in society, yes. The Vietnam War was raging. Student rebellion had spilled out into the city streets of what had normally been quiet college towns. Desegregation and the civil rights movement was in full swing. The United States had landed a manned spacecraft on the moon. It was clearly a period of deep and lasting changes. Nevertheless, the system operated by religious was at the base of the success of a good many other people.

Many, if not most, parish priests, for instance, did not support departure from the long-established procedures of women religious. Nor did many laypeople. After all, their parishes ran on the services of these women; their budgets depended on their presence, even in large, well-to-do, middle-class suburbs that had become accustomed to the basically free services of sisters to run the parish school or catechetical programs, to clean the churches and make the altar breads.

Public pressure to control or contain the updating of religious life was immense. Every week letters to the editor in Catholic newspapers criticized the movement of sisters from the schools into other ministries. Bishops warned of the dire consequences that would come with the "lack of respect" for sisters that would follow if the changes, especially of habit, continued. Some bishops, like Cardinal J. Francis McIntyre in Los

Angeles, attempted to permit only sisters in habits to work in their dioceses. Some priests hired only sisters in veils to teach in their schools, an attempt to bring economics to bear on theology.

Others, in Erie, for instance, when faced with requests from the women superiors of the diocese in the late 1970s to raise the monthly stipend of a teaching sister from $200 per month to $400 per month, insisted on seeing the community budget before agreeing to the increase. "If you wore habits instead of blouses," a diocesan official said, "you wouldn't need more money to live on. You could go on sacrificing for others as you are supposed to do." And Mary Margaret's answer was, "Father, give us the money and we'll decide for ourselves to whom to give our charity."

It was a moment suspended in time and writ in blood.

More than the public resisted the changes that were coming in religious life, however. Community members themselves balked. What many thought would be a kind of cosmetic approach to renewal turned out to be a full-scale review of everything in the life: the governance structures, the theology of the vows, community life, the formation program, the clothing, the prayer life, ministry — in fact, the entire constitution of the federation, the law by which Benedictine women of Erie had lived since 1922. Everything they had always known about life was now "experimental." Meaning uncertain. Meaning unorthodox. Meaning slipping away. Whole lifetimes of living were slipping away.

The 1968 General Chapter in accordance with the mandates of Vatican II opened the constitutions to experimentation and provided a model of social change to be envied. What it did not provide was a blueprint of how to help the people who were caught in the process, sometimes crushed in the process, because the changes were either too many — or too few.

What happened to the people became the defining issue in renewal, an insight into the struggle it took to stay faithful in a period of what appeared to be a time of organized infidelity, of deep disaffection.

15

Where Theory Ends

THE PEOPLE

I T'S VERY TEMPTING to talk about renewal in terms of cur-
rents in the culture or the need for theological development.
In fact, most of us do. But the fact under the fact is that renewal
was not an academic exercise, whatever its shapers thought.
The important thing to remember is that there was something
going on here that was more than history or theology. What
really fueled the struggles of the renewal period lay in what was
happening to the women themselves as one change either did
or did not follow the one before it.

In the first place, the twentieth century represents a fissure
in Western history. It was the cleavage point between two distinctly different realities. The world in the twentieth century
moved as inexorably into a technological world — a nuclear
one — from an industrial one as centuries before it had once
moved from agriculture to industry. The change each move
brought to the lives of those who straddled the two societies
affected the very character of both church and society.

The movement from agriculture to industry changed the
way farmers farmed. Small family farms gave way eventually to agribusinesses on vast tracts of land and huge pieces
of equipment and farm managers rather than farm owners.
The new agribusinesses led to huge profits for some farmers,
paid labor for some, and total loss of lands for others. Cities
swelled to twice their size. Family patterns changed and culture
with them.

The movement from industry to technology, accomplished in a much shorter period of time but with just as much impact, changed the way people lived as well as how they made their living, changed the way they saw society and changed the way they defined themselves as well. Families spread out over the face of the earth and at the same time stayed connected now by computers. Distance became an attitude of mind rather than a measurement. Industries moved, too, to where other peoples would go on doing manual labor, less skilled labor, while one class of people in the United States worked on mainframes in cyberspace and another flipped hamburgers at McDonalds or serviced the self-help machines that turned the country into a capital-intensive economy. A new generation of college educated suburbanites, of which there were now many, earned their money in finance or in information processing companies or by providing health care or personal services rather than on assembly lines and by hard physical labor. A white-collar world developed white-collar ideals.

And all of this happened in less than twenty-five years. The United States of America went into World War I one kind of nation and came out of World War II completely another.

Change was a given in such a society — except in those places like monasteries, convents, and churches that had been built on the very ideals of changelessness and stability. While the world had gone mad around them — in the rudderless Middle Ages, in the political fluctuations of the feudal era, despite the breakdown of the unity of the church, through one war after another — they had remained, in large part, rooted in the past.

Religious wanted change, too, of course, but up to this time change, real change, had never actually been the conscious issue. Most people didn't really want change at all. And certainly not in the church. They wanted adjustments that would make being different possible as long as their world stayed basically the same. They wanted a little less pressure here, a little loosening up there. Nothing all that serious.

Change, in fact, loomed unthinkable in groups whose underlying value was that whatever the hysteria in the society around them, they had persevered. They had been true to the original vision. They had not wavered.

The basic image of the religious institution was fidelity, stability, and calm. To shatter all of that, to be faithful but different at the same time, seemed impossible. The certainty emanating from years of magisterial teaching gave a sense of total rightness to the institution. What could possibly need to be changed in an institution that "had always been that way."

Then Vatican II mandated the review of the constitutions of every religious order in the church with an eye to "renewal."

It was in this kind of institutional climate that delegates to the Renewal Chapters of 1968 began the work of reviewing the constitutional norms in accordance with its founding intention, the needs of the members, and the character of the age in which it existed. The cavernous distance among these elements takes the breath away. Even now. And the most fascinating of all is that so few recognized the consequence to their communities of the distances among them.

These were delegates who, by virtue of being American, were more accustomed to shifts in the social landscape than many. It never seems to have occurred to them that in closed communities such as theirs they needed to have as much respect for the psychology of the event as they did its theological underpinnings. They needed psychological preparation for change in groups for which change was a foreign land. They needed psychological help to make the life transitions such changes would involve at least as much as they needed footnotes from the new theological documents to chart the new directions. Instead, the federation chapter worked on the theology of renewal. They left the psychology of it to each local community.

Discussions at the level of the General Chapter explored ideas and wrestled with heady concepts like the theology of the vows — was "poverty" now, for instance, what "poverty" had been when its canonical formulations were first devised? Discussions at the local level, on the other hand, very often took a completely different turn. Here the living out of the vow brought communities face-to-face with some of the oldest practices in the order. Could sisters have money in their pockets? Could sisters buy their own personal supplies? Could sisters have credit cards? Could sisters save for major purchases like coats or boots, for instance, now that they weren't wearing capes anymore or buying the same kinds of shoes from the same stores anymore? And if they could, what happened to the notion of a vow at all? Some communities, rich in intellectual heritage or variety of ministries, negotiated the challenge well. Others, isolated both geographically and professionally, were torn apart. The monastery in Erie fell somewhere in between.

Three psychological dimensions of social change were almost completely overlooked during renewal: the problems of human security, identity, and belief in a person's freedom to change. If anything, issues such as these were at least ignored, if not dismissed, as inconsequential or immature. The relationship between the intellectual and the psychological had never been of high priority in religious communities. Emotional needs were, by and large, simply spiritualized. People learned to "offer things up," to "have faith," to "trust God," to "do the will of God" which, translated, meant to "obey" the current directive in hopes of eternal reward.

The spiritual life concentrated, for the most part, on the intellectual dimensions of the life: formal prayers, theological development, professional proficiency, the vows. How change would effect the membership psychologically, therefore, was of very minor interest, at least at the beginning of renewal. Erie was a basically young community and brought to the problems of renewal both energy and inexperience. The period became an amalgam of both. The community had yet to discover the difference between the adoption of a change and the internalization of a change.

The change model adopted was itself a simple and efficient one: the community was organized into study groups related to the various areas of religious life — prayer, ministry, governance, community, and the vowed life.

The mandate given to each study group was clear: they were to study the Vatican documents by comparing the concepts and assumptions there to the theology or practice of the life as they knew it. Then they were to present to the community whatever recommendations for change they considered necessary to bring the two theologies into conjunction. Once the chapter voted to accept the recommendations, the community would begin to put the new practices into effect.

On the surface, the method was a cogent one. But it was not easy. Change, we discovered the hard way, is a process, not an event. For some people change is intuited; for others change must be chosen. What's more, change and changes are not always the same thing. Changes in the way we go about a thing, modifications of basic behaviors — using a truck rather than a horse to pull a caisson — leaves my world and the way I function in it basically intact. Change, real change, stands to turn my whole world upside down.

Change, the adoption of a new worldview, threatens the psyche to the point of psychological collapse. It toys with emotional disequilibrium. It effects who we ourselves think we are. It touches my core beliefs, it threatens my emotional security, it changes my very definition of self. People who change cultures or religions or social theories can find themselves swimming in a sea of uncertainty for years. Expatriates can go through life wondering if they really belong anywhere. Converts are never sure they really have it right. People raised to believe in the grandeur of the human race feel their hubris wilt in the face of the immensity of the universe, the implications of the new science.

The problem with the process of renewal, therefore, lay in the fact that the process took little or no note of the internal dynamics of change, except at one level. In most cases, no one was required to do what the new theses allowed. No one was required to wear contemporary clothes, no one was required to leave teaching, no one was expected to create the liturgies that would incorporate the newly approved prayer forms.

At the same time, women who had not done personal shopping for up to fifty years, suddenly had to get themselves to stores and choose among sizes and styles and brands that confused them. Sisters who loved teaching school but found themselves the last religious in schools with dwindling populations lived in fear of not being able to find another position if this one ended. Sisters who had recited the psalms from memory for years found themselves stumbling through new translations, bereft at the loss of the comforting old hymns, appalled by all the noise at Mass.

A sense of personal security, psychological identity, and fundamental beliefs, all basic to a healthy sense of self, struggled for new direction. Is this right? What do I believe about life? Who am I now? These were core questions that would all need to be answered again one at a time. Slowly, slowly, slowly.

16

The Burning Question of Identity

A T MOMENTS OF GREAT CHANGE, distinct personality types often find themselves at odds about how to go about it. In Erie the differences were plain. Women of great ability but deeply discordant ideas about the basics of life saw the challenges of renewal from very unlike perspectives. As the process went plunging forward intellectually and above the fray of fears and feelings, they grappled, both within themselves and together, to get a foothold on the process that would itself symbolize that their lives were still sensible, still sound, still under control.

High intuits, whose vision of the future was deeply perceptive but seldom clearly articulated, simply "knew" that renewal was necessary and were intent on the now of it.

High sensates, whose approach to the present bordered on the visceral, understood the pressing reasons for immediate change, took them for granted, and were confused by the need to keep repeating what they found to be obvious.

On the other hand, the rationalists in every group, who needed arguments on which to rest their justification for change, either slowed the process by pursuing one question after another or, satisfied that the theology of change was clear, insisted on its implementation. No more theorizing, no more argument.

Finally, those who needed order and the opportunity to judge issues on the basis of results and who needed to evaluate changes one at a time before they moved on to a new phase of the process felt swept away by the rate of change.

The link between what the social psychologist called "the intuitive" and "the rational" broke down. Things were done "because." The reasons given were invariably intellectual or pragmatic. For those who needed logical linkages or emotional authorization, the pace of change was indefensibly dangerous. The connection between the rational foundation and the emotional effects of such changes on the members themselves were more likely minimized in such an intellectual culture, if not discounted entirely.

As a result, the need for an institution to send out clear signals about what it was about, why it existed, why it was good for other people that it exist went by the wayside. And the lack of public definition undermined internal morale and public magnetism. Sisters ceased to be a sign of the joy of the life. Prospective members ceased to see a reason to enter a group whose identity had overnight become so badly blurred, so generally in question. The number of vocations declined. The questions about religious life increased. The ability of the members themselves to justify their own lifestyle diminished. Interestingly enough, *Insights*, a community publication planned for the express purpose of explaining to the various publics of the community — friends, families, benefactors, clergy — the nature and purpose of the changes that were daily more and more apparent in the life of the Erie Benedictines never saw the light of day. The community itself, understandably, could not agree on common statements to explain the changes in lifestyle and direction. Or, if statements could be written, they could not be universally maintained. Before the ink was dry on the page, new ideas or new directions had either ended or emerged too quickly to be explained. Erie was a community groaning in the wind.

Issues of security, identity, fidelity, and frustration plagued the group and eroded the image of the community as "community" outside and in, inside as well as out.

Members struggled with questions of security. The questions that ate at their lives day in and day out were, Am I being faithful to what I vowed I would do? And what will happen to me if I am not?

For older members of the community the "higher vocation/ hell and damnation" theology on which they had been raised did not disappear either easily or quickly. They were no longer sure who or what they were.

Younger members, on the other hand, who had never much internalized the traditional works or concepts to begin with saw another world entirely. That was the world with which they wanted to identify, not with a medieval memory of a grand and glorious tradition. After all, they reasoned, if Benedictinism could not be translated to this culture, why have it at all?

The questions of parents, the skepticism of families, the doubts of the priests with whom they worked corroded the sense of certainty that had been a hallmark of a sister's entire religious life. These religious conformed to the changes that were made, but they were never completely, never fully, convinced of the rightness of what they were doing. These were women, remember, whose own professional theological backgrounds had been purposely made thin.

More difficult than the security issues, however, the identity question went straight to the heart of the problem. The habit, the long, black medieval garb of heavy wool with its straight scapular, high linen head gear, and veil, made Benedictine women anonymous and, ironically, made them distinctive at the same time. They stood out in every crowd. The question was "who" stood out in every crowd. Every woman in the community was simply "sister." There were no last names used and few baptismal names either. A "name in religion" given at the time of entrance to the novitiate erased whatever was left of the "person" who had entered. To change the habit then was both to take away an old identity and give a new identity at the same time.

The problem was that few sisters had any real idea, after years of anonymity, who they were as individuals anymore. That life, that world, that person had been put down years before. In fact, putting it down had been part and parcel of the purpose and value of the life. The very thought of taking it up again, of having to figure out how to be a separate human being with an identity of one's own, an identity that had more to it than the stamp of an institution, bordered on the unthinkable.

With the identity question came the "respect" question. "If you people stop wearing habits," priest after priest warned us, "you will lose all the respect you get from the children and their parents." We were not, it seems, respected as people; we were respected as some kind of religious artifact. How that explained the respect given to doctors or ministers or public school teachers, no one ever said. But the questions under the question were real: Who would we be when we weren't ecclesiastical icons anymore? Was there anything left in us that could possibly stand alone?

And what about "witness"? We were in habits to witness, we were told. But exactly what it was to which we were witnessing became more and more blurred as the answers failed to satisfy the question. Were we witnessing to Benedictinism itself because, if so, most people didn't really know one habit from the next. In fact, nuns didn't know one habit from the next. As part of Notre Dame's annual summer school picnic for the more than fifteen hundred sister-students on campus in 1965, I organized a "style show" of a hundred different religious from a hundred different orders or their variations. I gave prizes to the sisters who could correctly identify the largest number of habits. Top prize went to a nun who recognized seven of the hundred different garbs modeled that day.

Everyone in the hall knew that we had just deconstructed one of the strongest arguments left against renewal, that change would blur the witness value of our orders. The truth, it seemed, was that the distinctive habits that were supposedly reminding the world of the various spiritual gifts of our congregations weren't really very distinctive at all. Not even to us.

The most interesting thing of all, perhaps, is that I myself was deeply attached to the habit at that time. By the end of the picnic, I and the almost fifteen hundred other nuns in the dining room that night had no choice but to go back to our rooms and rethink the whole question of the witness value of a habit.

If it was Jesus we were witnessing to, it began to occur to us that this was the Jesus who refused to give anybody a sign, the Jesus who had become "like us in all things, save sin." What's more, for some reason, the so-called witness value of the habit seemed to repel as many people as it attracted. Including Catholics.

Finally, if it was a kind of public availability, a connectedness to the human race, to which we were witnessing, it was also true that though many people did talk to us in public, little that was said could really be counted as genuine communication. People by and large talked to nuns at a distance: distant from the reality of their real concerns, distant from the world and its questions, distant from the human condition. It was plastic or pious talk, but, in most cases, not real person-to-person talk. We simply weren't real people to them. A five-year-old child brought to the convent office to wait for his working mother stared at the sister-portress thoughtfully for a while. Then the little boy got up, walked over behind the desk at which she sat, looked her up and down from her heavy black shoes to the high tipped coronet on her head and said slowly, "Are you a mommy — or a daddy — or a book?" So much for witnessing to children.

Clearly, dehumanization had set in where witness was supposed to have been.

But it was who we were, and the very thought of having to come out from behind all of that to become, well, nothing, brought the whole purpose of the life into question. Brought the whole purpose of their own life into question. Which was, of course, another problem.

For those who had literally given up everything — family, personal freedom, economic security, human comforts — who had sacrificed their wills, their creativity, their identity, their very selves in a world where those things were becoming ever more desirable, ever more attainable, renewal had to have been fraught with pain. For some, the pain came out of the desire to bring those things back to life in them. For others, though, the pain came out of knowing that to go back to those things now, in any degree, was tantamount to admitting that it had been foolish, purposeless — if not ethically questionable and psychologically unwise — to have given them up in the first place. The loss of self simply had to be justified or the rest of their lives had been wasted. Their choices had been wrong. They had been foolish. There was no way to prove that their first decisions had been right except by not accepting another one. They held on. They refused to change. When everyone around them moved beyond the point of stalemate, began at least to make adjustments, they held fast to the past that had made them.

The frustration that came out of all this turmoil hung thick over every gathering, every conversation, every session of the community chapter. Some people were holding the line with all their might. Others were restless to get on with the process, to become a new kind of woman religious in a new kind of church. They were tired of the dallying, disgusted with the wrangling, depressed by the tension of it all. "I just want you people to know," the young sister sitting on the grass in the convent yard said tersely and to no one in particular at the end of one especially bruising meeting, "I can't wait around here forever for something to happen." And few did. In the late 1960s, the bottom fell out of the scholasticate, the preparation stage before final profession. Now there was not only no clearly defined present, but there was no future to be seen either.

The problems of renewal, at least to some degree, were the same for laypeople as they were for nuns. People left parishes because guitars were used where once only the organ had been. The loss of high altars, the removal of statues, the lifting of the

ban against eating meat on Fridays — a practice which they
told us had sent more than a few people to hell — left the
Catholic population confused, disturbed, even angry. But these
people did not have to live together as religious communities
did. They did not have to deal with the issues at every meal,
in every ministry, in every house in the system. They left the
church and shrugged their shoulders or left one church and
went looking for another church in which the style of worship
suited them better. Religious could not do that. Religious could
not run and hide. They could only stay and struggle or leave
and feel betrayed. "I did not leave religious life," I told my
mother and father while I tried to figure out what to do next.
"Religious life left me."

Polarization set in. An organization, social scientists tell us,
is only a group of groups. Without people who have membership or acceptance in more than one of the component groups,
the group as a whole cannot survive.[7] Erie, like many communities, parishes, and dioceses around it, fragmented into
tightly drawn enclaves. Discovering how to bridge the gap between groups, determining how to put the whole group back
together again, seemed impossible.

17

Chaos and Creativity

Two issues, in particular, gave testimony to the character
of Mary Margaret's whole administration. She took very
seriously what the Vatican documents defined as the criteria
of authentic renewal. First, however difficult the financial or
internal environment in the community, she never lost sight of
"the needs of the members." Second, she stood in the center of
the community totally open to the "signs of the times." Most
of all, she never used one criterion as an excuse to abandon
the other.

Mary Margaret Kraus had believed in renewal from the very
beginning. A totally committed woman with a free spirit herself, she saw no reason to herd people into doing what they had
freely pledged themselves to do. Her approach to everything,
even in this period of challenge and change, was quiet and easy.
The times, the person, and the task were right for each other.

Theorists were beginning to call the phenomenon "synergy,"
the working together of two or more things to produce an effect
greater than the sum of their parts. In her, the quiet manner,
the deep commitment gave credibility to change. The combination was rare. It wasn't always the case everywhere that
leadership was so willing to both lead and be led at the same
time. In Erie it became the key to a new beginning.

In fact, in 1968 Mary Margaret had already signaled the possibility of new beginnings by launching a capital campaign for
the purpose of building a new monastery. And this in the face of
the uncertain future of religious life in general. Most religious
pundits were sure that within ten years there would be no such

thing as religious life, and if any of it did still exist, it would be found only in small isolated groups, groups too small for large monasteries. This was surely no time to be building one.

The community had felt the burden of the old house for years, actually. There was no real infirmary there, few bathroom facilities, no private sleeping spaces, and even the refectory, the community dining room, was too small to seat and serve the entire community at once.

Alice herself had begun to consider the idea of building a new monastery but, given her illness and the uncertainty surrounding a site for it, never pursued the subject through to the end. Instead, Mary Margaret found herself with no choice but to begin building. Insurance companies notified the community that they would no longer cover the old wood and brick structure in the middle of the city where a number of older sisters were housed.

But simply rebuilding the oldest section of the house was hardly the answer to the whole problem. The great exodus had not yet begun. The community, it seemed, was becoming larger and more crowded every year. Sisters home from diocesan teaching positions for the summer were now sleeping fifteen at a time in what, during the school year, were high school classrooms. And last but most significant of all, perhaps, the city had finally extended the gas, water, and electric utilities to the land the community had owned on East Lake Road since 1906. Development of that property was finally possible.

Then, in 1969, with the building project well under way, at the second session of its Renewal Chapter, the Federation of Saint Scholastica — an association of prioresses and delegates from twenty-three member monasteries — opened 27 of the 101 articles of the constitutions to "experimentation" on the basis of the theological study papers submitted by the research committees of the chapter.

At this point, with the General Chapter attending to the first Vatican criterion, "the charism of the founder," local monasteries concentrated on the other two dimensions of renewal, "the needs of the members and the signs of the times." Building a new monastery only added meaning to the process.

Suddenly, however, the community found itself near bankruptcy. Steel prices had risen in the process of the capital campaign and building costs soared. Now there was tension inside the community and danger from without as well. Mary Margaret simply got up at the next General Chapter of the federation, tears in her eyes, knowing that we would have no money coming in till the end of September, and asked for financial help. The tears were part of her personality; the situation was not part of Erie's history. Erie had always been a frugal community, but "frugal" and being unable to pay your bills or buy food for the community in the summertime are two different things.

Like all nuns in those days, sisters were paid by the month for the ten months out of the year in which they taught in the Catholic school system. During the summer months, they relied on the community festival to handle the grocery bills. Doctors gave free services and families provided the rest. But with the coming of compulsory medical insurance, compulsory automobile insurance, compulsory mortgage protection insurance, and rising utility bills, $200 a month per sister could not possibly handle that and a rising mortgage too. The member priories of the federation, difficult as their own situations were, produced low-interest or no-interest loans and, in her characteristic way, Mary Margaret simply went on. She curbed none of the experiments in progress, cautioned no one to imagine less, trusted that since the situations we were in were not of our own making, they had to be of God's making so God would surely see us through. Somehow, someday. Maybe not the way we would have planned it or liked it but certainly the way it was meant to be.

Now renewal had begun for the Erie Benedictines at every possible level — physically, theologically, and socially.

As prioress, Mary Margaret brought two gifts to the renewal process: a listening heart and a naturally loving personality. The combination lacks the ring of corporate effectiveness, perhaps, but, in the end, it saved the Erie Benedictines, not organizationally — meaning efficiently — but spiritually, meaning physically whole and spiritually intact.

Leadership where Mary Margaret was concerned had more to do with supporting the group while it found its own way than with driving the group to her own solutions. She did not come to a community chapter with answers, with decisions she had decided to have the chapter "approve." She came to the community with honest questions and trusted that the wisdom of the community would find the best possible answers to them. It was a slow process and a rocky one. It was also a profoundly regenerating one.

Mary Margaret had no background in "process," in the capacity to raise, examine, evaluate, and arrive at decisions together. But she trusted those who did. No authoritarian would have allowed such a thing. As a result of it, however, though the Erie Benedictines moved through renewal reluctantly in part and with difficulty always, they moved through it together. They explored every idea, heard every concern, considered every amendment, were faced with every nuance, listened to everyone, and then went on together. It wasn't pretty but it was real. It tested every ounce of community commitment a woman ever thought she had. Community meetings were long and painful in those days. People were not afraid to say what they thought, and what they thought came out of either fear or frustration.

The freedom of the format, however, allowed people to identify their own concerns and wrestle with the answers, even if they didn't like them, even if they couldn't own them yet. Nothing was repressed, everyone was to speak. Every meeting got worse than the one before it, either because at one meeting things were happening too slowly for some or, at the next, things were going too quickly for others. Hostility was high. Personal mistrust was high. Hope was low.

Mary Margaret steered through the worst of the storm by giving individuals permission to do what the majority of the group was not ready to agree ought to be. She kept every answer open until the group had the experience to make a final decision on it. The majority of the community, for instance, did not agree that individuals should be permitted to live in houses or apartments in town despite the fact that the community had a history of living in small group parish missions for over seventy-five years. The problem was that those living situations had been on "church property." These new living situations would be in privately owned houses. Those early missions had been for the sake of a community activity, parish teaching. These new living situations had no institutional goal except presence to the people. The first parish living situations, supplied by the congregations, cost the community only the amount they needed for food and personal expenses. These experimental living arrangements would be at community expense, an unheard of notion in those days, and for no clearly defined community task. After all, staying away from the "world" was the ideal, not moving in with it.

Furthermore, these new groups would be coming together out of common concerns or interests, not simply because of work. They would be self-selecting groups, not appointed ones. The early missions had been "religious." They existed for the sake of the Catholic community. These new concerns were "secular." They would be relating to residents of regular neighborhoods for no specific institutional reason at all. And "institutional" is all we had ever been.

The community deadlocked over the issue. And a plethora of other ones as well: ministries, clothing, public involvement, and personal freedoms. In her wisdom and her perception of individual needs, Mary Margaret simply gave permission to open an apartment in town and waited for experience to dictate to the community at large whether such a move was a good one for "the people of God" or not. It linked the role of the prioress with the role of the chapter in ways seldom seen in modern history. The community chapter set policy after long and deep discussion and debate; the prioress allowed exception to it after great prayer and deep concern for the person.

Everyone participated in every issue. As a result, perhaps, instead of moving to the margins at the time of stress, the usual response when groups feel threatened with the inevitable, they stayed in the process and worked it out. They were in the center of the process and they knew it. In fact, they were the process.

Mary Margaret went through one conflict, one personality clash at a time, in the same evenhanded way. And she never said stop, she never aborted the process, she never resisted the growth that came from struggle.

The new process was painful. Authoritarianism can be so much easier than personal participation. Authoritarian governments give us all someone to blame when things go wrong. Participative governments require us to take responsibility for ourselves. Without the personal participation she allowed to take root in a community that for centuries had been built on total chapter involvement in group decision-making, Erie would have been driven through renewal. Instead, Erie was led through renewal.

Without the openness that welcomed every possible idea, every potential project, every personal fear, and encouraged every raging hope that we might be as much a part of tomorrow as we had been of yesterday, the future could never possibly have come for us. Renewal would at most have been a dusting off of the past, a superficial approach to questions that touched the very core of the life.

Scholars have known for decades that social norms are the matrix, the center, out of which lasting attitudes and behaviors spring. It's not possible to change social norms, core beliefs, without touching the deepest feelings a person has, not only about herself but about every single object, person, group, or institution around her. What I believe dictates what I do.

The more committed a person is to something, the more her ego, her own self-system, is tied up with the nature of a group or an idea about the world, the more consistent she is socially. To know what group a person belongs to, to know what a person believes about even one central issue, is to be able to predict a great deal about that person. To know that a person is Catholic or Mormon or Muslim, a war veteran, a stock broker, a woman, for instance, brings with it a whole constellation of insights and understandings about that person.

The dark side of such predictions is, of course, stereotypes and prejudices. At the same time, these perceptions help a person to know what can and cannot be talked about in the office, for instance, without causing tension.

Core beliefs about God and the self are among the most difficult of all to reshape because they have to do with a person's place, not only among a single people, but about a person's very place in the universe. Theologians tell us that it takes almost a hundred years for a council of the church to be "received." The reasons are clear. People grow into core beliefs. They also have to grow out of the old ones before social change can be considered final.

Religious communities, and certainly the Erie Benedictines, found themselves plunged into a struggle for which they had no name. Disagreements on core beliefs about God, self, vows, church, and women masking simply as lifestyle adjustments were the unrecognized ghost in every discussion.

More than that, various members of the community, at all age levels, were more or less committed to these core beliefs. The young had been witnessing to them for far fewer years. They came from a society, from homes, that had, at least tacitly, questioned them for years. They kept the rules but they did not internalize them. They "spoke fault" for breaking them but they did not repent. They said the words but they did not really believe things that the generations before them did. It was ritual for them, not belief. Scrupulosity was not a disease of this new generation.

Other members, on the other hand, whose piety at home had been just as church-centered, just as sin-laden, just as self-effacing as that of most of the women of their day and age, were more likely to distrust the new, but unspoken, assumptions of Vatican II, at least where their own lives were concerned. For them, the major changes that came out of renewal compromised the very meaning of their lives. No wonder that their renewal became a tug of war, not between two lifestyles, but between two ways of looking at the purpose, the core, of religious life, two ways of looking at what religious life must really be about.

In communities made up largely of an older generation, the pace of change was slow, the boundaries of change were clearer. In Erie, where the median age at the beginning of the renewal period was fifty-two, the pressure for change was high. Change was a head-long attempt to catch the future before it was too late. It was Mary Margaret Kraus's laser-like attention to the needs of the members and the signs of the times that provided the stars to steer by toward tomorrow.

18

Faith and Frustration

The stories of fear, frustration, and simple faith that memorialize Mary Margaret's administration and this middle period of renewal are endless. Each of them deals with a core belief about God, self and the world that did not go quietly away.

One of the unspoken but clearly defined core beliefs of religious life lay in the notion that "obedience" was its cornerstone. Obedience to a superior on earth demonstrated the human being's surrender to the will of God in heaven, we were told. Obedience, therefore, had to do with an unthinking response to unexplained, even irrational, commands. The less resistance, the fewer the questions, the truer the virtue. Mary Margaret, on the other hand, looked at the documents of Vatican II and never doubted that the whole church, "the people of God," were being called to moral responsibility rather than to some kind of unthinking reflex action.

But the tensions of renewal seemed endless, touched every dimension of the life, left no place to hide, nowhere to rest, no way to reach across the boundaries of social change to the friendships that had once existed, the camaraderie that once marked everything we did together, the oneness of mind that seemed once to prevail.

Another of the core beliefs of religious life revolved around the notion that prayer was "conversation with God." Prayer was the beginning of communion with the Divine. It was done on a higher plane than human conversation. The idea was centuries old. Teresa of Avila, for instance, faced a threat from the Spanish Inquisition because her prayer had been defined as "too personal" and therefore Protestant. The new document on the liturgy, on the other hand, broadened both the form and the nature of prayer. Formulas got a great deal less emphasis than older Roman documents were wont to define; relevance and participation got a great deal more. Prayer was just as central, just as regular, but far less burdening. It was in English now, and it took an average of two to three hours a day rather than four.

At the same time, this was a community denied the right to say the breviary for years because Benedictine sisters were no longer "cloistered" as European nuns had been and therefore, in the canonical terms of that era, did not qualify to say the Divine Office. They were given the "Little Office of the Blessed Virgin," instead, a gesture that did not go down well with Benedictines. What's more, this was a community so poor that when they did receive permission to say the Office in 1908 they had to beg for years for castoff breviaries from male monasteries with which to do it. Having contended so long for the right to say the Office, the very thought of changing it, reducing it, touched deep, deep chords, church documents or no church documents. Not surprisingly then, prayer, too, became a battleground.

Free now to develop new prayer forms, we used dance and drama one evening at Vespers to bring a more dynamic interpretation of the readings into the Divine Office. Sister Ignatia, past prioress and grand old Flemish woman whose needs for order and formula were as straight as her backbone, simply got up and, with four other sisters following her, walked sternly, solemnly out of chapel. "If you call that prayer," she said as she left, "I apologize to Almighty God."

At the end of Vespers, a young sister went to her room: "Sister Ignatia," she said, "I want you to know that I love you. But I did not respect you for leaving chapel during the dance. The Divine Office means as much to those dancers as it does to you." Sister Ignatia looked long and hard at the young woman — her sincerity, her passion, her pain — and perhaps knowing that the tide had turned, the day was lost, said simply, "I will put a seal upon my lips." No doubt about it: every generation in the community was in some kind of pain.

In Oil City, one of the community missions, a young local superior of a house full of older members — the Four-Horsemen-of-the-Community types — came home to the parish convent one night after school to find one of the newly ordained curates of the parish unscrewing the communion rail in the convent chapel. "And I was left to explain it to them," she remembers with a sigh.

Another of the core beliefs of religious life revolved around "transcendence," the notion that religious withdrew from the "temptations of the world" to live a life of perfection and union with God. It was a spirituality of disengagement in an age and a community that was at the same time deeply engaged in the business of the day. Just as the Pastoral Constitution on the Church in the Modern World had implied it should be.

In Erie, sisters came home from school every night to find the latest note on the community bulletin board about the "true" nature of monasticism — all of them unsigned. "I was so distraught," a young sister said later. "I wanted to leave." Two theologies of religious life, one made out of the clay of the ascetical tradition (the mystique of religious life), the other out of the theology of transformation (the scandal of the incarnation), grappled day after day for ascendency.

Mary Margaret took notes off of bulletin boards and never said a word. She explained changes to pastors and never backed off from insisting on the right of the community to determine its own experiments in lifestyle. When Bishop John Francis Whealon tried to forbid the movement of sisters into houses or apartments in town, Mary Margaret, a quiet woman, contested his interference in the internal life of the community, an arena over which even bishops had no canonical control. Bishop Whealon, a powerful man, backed down.

Then Bishop Whealon, having seen and disapproved of the projected changes in the Erie Benedictines, came to the community himself to instruct the sisters on the theology of religious life. He made the point of saying that Rome had already defined the universal meaning of the vows, that the definitions of poverty, chastity and obedience were already carved in stone and could not be interpreted otherwise.

Mary Margaret got up and from the center of the community and said, "Bishop, I didn't take vows of poverty, chastity, and obedience." The bishop, with no small amount of exasperation said, "Of course you did, Sister. If you didn't take vows of poverty, chastity, and obedience, you can't be a religious." Mary Margaret, prioress of the community, gave him that sly smile of hers and said, "Then, Bishop, I'm not a religious. I took Benedictine vows: obedience, stability, and conversion of life." The community could hardly suppress the laugh that played on every face, sparkled in every eye.

The point was clear now for everyone to see: bishops did not know everything about religious life and therefore could not dictate to it. The renewal of religious life was up to religious. The meeting ended, the renewal process went on, the bishop never asked for another meeting again at which to teach religious life to religious.

One of the most disputed of the core values of pre–Vatican II religious life was the notion of witness, that to be religious was to be visibly present to the rest of the church as "set apart," "consecrated," "special." Even the clothing of a nun was blessed. But though the habit was indeed a witness, the question was to what, and the answer had become blurred. Out of touch with the styles of the time, it frightened small children and repulsed Protestants. It made movement into public ministry impossible in a country dedicated to the separation of church and state, and in a society marked by the decline of the Catholic school system itself, it threatened the very livelihood of teaching communities. Unless they could become integrated into the society around them, they could hardly minister to it; unless they could become incarnated in the world, they could find the leaven of their lives limited to very small areas of life.

Two issues in renewal touched the lay community, however, almost as profoundly as it touched the religious community itself. The first pertained to the habit; the second to open placement. Public pressure built up around both of these and divided the community itself deeply.

All the arguments aside for being an "incarnational presence in society," for being immersed in the life of the age rather than withdrawn from it, there were problems with the change of habit that had nothing to do with theology. Sisters who had been in community for years, who had not combed or styled their hair for decades, who had not chosen so much as socks since they were teenagers found themselves having to find and fit and choose clothes. Those who had families, sisters, from whom to get help were the lucky ones. Others found themselves adrift, embarrassed, and stripped of their dignity, let alone confused by the new theology that prompted the relinquishment of dress that stretched over centuries.

Jesus himself never took on any of the essential signs of religious witness common to his culture, never wore distinguishing dress, was not part of the priestly tribe of Levites, was not even a rabbi, in the strict sense of the word. But over the years the incarnational aspect of the life of Jesus had given way to the theology of transcendence. As a result religious dress, which had once been forbidden but over the years had become common, found itself under inspection again. To ease the difficulty of a clothing change, Mary Margaret organized a style show for the community.

The idea was that sisters would model new designs of habits or headgear to get the community to begin to think in terms of modern modifications of what had been the dress of European women in the early Middle Ages.

One sister redesigned the coif and headdress. Another sister eliminated the coif entirely and shortened the veil. Another sister shortened the habit. A fourth sister appeared in a jacket top over a black dress. The last sister to model a possible new habit, Sister Mary Regina Flanagan, was the oldest sister in the program. She came on stage wearing her sister's green suit. First, the community gasped. Then it began to dawn on them: experimentation meant experimentation. Change was more than adjustment. And, most of all, perhaps, the desire for renewal — not simply the warmed-over remnants of an earlier age — crossed every age barrier. What they were about was a theological and social phenomenon, not an exercise in historical repair.

Shortly after the change from medieval dress to simple dark suits in the style of the day, I was at a parish Mass on a Sunday. Suddenly, the sister I was with, ten years my senior, discovered a run in her hose. She sat rooted to the pew, tight and gray-faced. Communion time came and went. She never moved. In the car later, angry and frustrated, she burst into tears. The strain of becoming a whole new person in a whole new community in a whole new church drained spirits dry. For many, tears came easily. Anger went deep. For others, the very need to spend so much time on the issue of clothes left little energy for the larger matters of renewal. "We made clothes and prayer equally important," one sister said. "Amazing when you think about it now."

But though some laypeople understood and applauded the changes, others were just as confused as some of the sisters themselves. To see sisters who were not in habits demanded changes in their own view of religious life and church. It was the sign that their own religious ghetto had broken down, that we were all in this world together, that we were all responsible for living the gospel in the modern world. The old notion that nuns and monks were responsible for praying the rest of the church out of purgatory disappeared with the disappearance of the mystique of religious life. The shock of it was only too clear.

One year, for instance, the community left classrooms for the Christmas vacation dressed in black serge and reappeared in their classrooms in January in skirts and hair-dos. For parishioners who wanted nothing to do with Vatican II, the change had all the effect of a cold wind on a winter morning. The feelings rippled through families from one end to the other. When young Joe Wisniewski came into the high school office to pay his tuition fees for the second term, for instance,

he shifted nervously from leg to leg, pushed the tuition envelope back and forth across the office counter, answered Sister
Maureen's questions about the family Christmas in monosyl-
lables, and stared down at his feet. "What is the matter with
that boy?" Maureen asked when he'd gone. "I have never seen
him look like that before." I winced. "No," I corrected her. "The
problem is that *he* has not seen *you* look like *that* before," I
said pointing at her head. "Apparently the only thing we have
managed to do in fifteen hundred years is to make a hairline
obscene."

Priests were particularly hostile to the change. Father Theobald, the pastor of Fryburg, made a point of looking around at
the sister staff and then, eyeing the one still in a veil, would say,
"I have only one sister in this house." After hearing the remark
one too many times, a sister answered back, "Father Theobald,
you were the only priest I ever saw without a Roman collar
when I came here and I never respected you any less for that. I
expect the same." Conversations about renewal with the clergy
were a tinder box. Robert Frost, the poet, once wrote, "Home is
where when you go there, they have to take you in." Nuns came
to understand that Frost was not universally, necessarily right.

In the middle of it all, the community passed one resolution after another about the nature of community dress. First,
sisters were required to wear black suits, white blouses, and a
short veil in all professional situations. But soon everybody had
a different definition of exactly what a "professional situation"
was. Did it mean in school only? Or when doing church work
as well? Or when answering the convent door? What? When?

Then some sisters wanted to wear colored blouses. So the
community decided that pastels were acceptable. But what exactly constituted a "pastel"? How light was light? How dark
was dark? Soon pastels went by the wayside and colored
blouses took over.

Then black suits became the norm. But when Mary Margaret herself went to find a new black suit to wear at the
dedication of the new Mount St. Benedict Monastery on East

Lake Road, she discovered that dark blue suits were less expensive. Mary Margaret appeared at the ceremony in navy blue. Soon Mary Margaret announced that veils and colors and styles of clothing were left to the "individual sister's discretion." Uniformity had ceased to be the order of the day.

But if looking normal and human was difficult, open placement — the plan to have sisters apply for positions rather than be placed in positions like a collection of interchangeable parts — came to be even harder. The core belief endangered by open placement was the concept that religious piety depended on religious disposability, the notion that religious were pawns in the hands of the institution.

As a result, every sister was "placed" every year, without consultation, often without regard for certification or even professional preparation. As educational standards improved, the strain of that became unbearable for many. They went where they were sent, of course, but many came back either ill or soured for life.

Open placement was the attempt to enable sisters to be free of artificial restraints in order to develop their gifts and talents to the full. The idea, encouraged by the human development movement, was that a happy nun would be a more effective nun. Now suddenly, however, they found themselves with other kinds of questions.

Women who had never had to fear for a position suddenly did not know if they would have a position the following year or not. It all depended now on more than simply knowing that if you were assigned to a place they had to take you.

For religious, it depended on three things. It depended on performance evaluations. It depended on whether the pastor liked her or not. It depended on local needs.

For the pastor, a sister's return depended on five things: It depended on her evaluation of the working conditions as well as his evaluation of her performance. It depended on her interests. It depended on the way she felt she had been treated in the situation. It depended on what she herself thought she should be doing to live a gospel life. It depended on whether she considered the needs of this particular place to be more important than the needs of another parish or place or people. The old theology of nuns as interchangeable parts dissolved in midair.

Ministry, once a community responsibility, became an individual responsibility. What's more, what had been a teaching community simply because women who wanted to be religious were willing also to be teachers in order to do it changed almost overnight. The Benedictine Sisters of Erie branched out far beyond classrooms, far beyond the twelve diocesan schools they had once staffed.

Over the years sisters became spiritual directors, liturgists, counselors, nurses, church personnel, administrators, artists, retreat directors, consultants, peace and justice advocates, child care specialists, and social workers.

They began to move in public circles as well as Catholic ones. They opened programs for the inner-city poor and unemployed adults, for women in prisons and for women in rural areas, for gays and lesbians, rich and poor. They went where their particular gifts met particular local needs. One or another went from Colorado to Virginia, from Cleveland to Chicago, from Erie to points around the world. They followed the gifts of the members. Public presence became both a call to gospel witness and a serious responsibility.

The development did not come without stress. "We had never written a resumé," one sister explained. "We had no idea how to apply for a position or what we had to offer to anyone."

In an environment in which decision-making had been suppressed in the name of sanctity, the very thought of choosing to apply for a real position touched on the old concepts of self-will and obedience and "pride." "I'll never forget the day," one sister recalled, "when Mary Margaret said to me, 'I need a buffer in that place.... Would you be willing to think about going there?'" Thinking about anything, choosing one thing over another, being able to say "I'll think about it" took the human development of sisters to a new level. It meant that women religious, too, were meant to go to God as adults, not as perpetual children.

The belief system on which religious life had been built found itself in contest with a belief system that had come into the church, as Pope John XXIII wanted, "like fresh air." It broke through the cement of the ages like shafts of green grass. But it broke people as well.

Now the problems were not so much theological as they were personal. The changes were largely in place. It was commitment to them that was lacking. The new documents of the church had turned religious life upside down and the people who lived it as well. The question now lay in whether or not the single-heartedness of the community life they had known for years could ever be rebuilt.

19

Facing the Feelings,
Facing the Fear

THREE INCIDENTS in the history of renewal may have done more than any others to bring a new perspective to the way the Erie Benedictines saw religious life and their own role in it. The first was a wandering monk, the second was death, and the third was a building.

The wandering monk enabled the community to attend to the personal dimensions of renewal.

The Rule of Benedict is a simple document about simple things: community life, service, prayer, stewardship, reflection, governance, and hospitality. One of its most charming passages deals with the place of guests in the life of the monastery. "Whenever guests arrive," the Rule says, "let them be received as Christ and let them stay as long as they find things agreeable (chap. 53). . . . But, if by chance, they should criticize anything there, the abbot should realize that God may have sent them for that very purpose" (chap. 61). Or to put it plainly: sometimes outsiders can see things about us that we don't recognize ourselves. Take them seriously. The advice is sound. We know because we had such an outsider.

Ronald Fogarty, SM, Australian monk and clinical psychologist, became the guest who could articulate the love and understanding that Mary Margaret could only model in our midst.

Ronald was in the United States doing postdoctoral work in clinical psychology at the University of Chicago. He had been devoting himself to religious communities around the world, trying to help them overcome their fears of renewal, trying to enable them to hear one another, something that hadn't happened for years, if ever. Whether it would work or not would have been anybody's guess. Religious communities all over the country were seriously polarized. Many of them toyed with establishing new foundations or simply dividing the congregation completely.

New groups, splinter groups from larger houses, or intentional groups whose focus was different from those of religious orders before them were springing up everywhere. They gathered, in large part, around issues of peace and justice. Around the peace movement itself. Around concern for a new kind of poor. Around women's issues. Some of those who left established congregations discounted the impact of ancient orders entirely. Some of them discounted the church and its controls. These people wanted to live in intentional communities but preferred to ally themselves with noncanonical groups who were freer to move than those who were operating under some kind of canonical umbrella.

After Ronald did a session at the Federation General Chapter, Mary Margaret engaged him immediately to come and do the same kind of thing in Erie.

Brother Ronald opened his presentation in the dark of the St. Benedict Academy cafeteria, showing slides of one monastery after another around the world until the very sight of them palled. The community was getting restless. What was the point of all this? Suddenly, he turned the projector off, turned on the lights in the room, and said to the group at large, "Do you know what all those monasteries have in common?" He waited while we shifted in our chairs. "They were all great abbeys at one time. They are all dead or dying now." The message was clear: "There but for the grace of God go we." Unless. The myth of immutability disappeared before our eyes.

Ronald came back to the community three times. The first time he talked about the nature of change. The second time he talked about the process of consensus. The third time he talked about human development.

But more than teach, he listened. He lectured for hours every day, yes, but then listened between conferences, during meals, through half the night working with one individual after another. He got to know them. He listened to their fears, their anger, their frustrations, their desires to be a community again.

The community loved him. Most of all, they trusted him. He looked ancient and gaunt and weathered. This was no theological rebel, no mindless young defector from the path of the straight and narrow. And, hearing the word through a stranger who knew their feelings and cared about their getting swept away by them, they got it. "Community" we finally figured out, was not about uniformity, not about geography. Community was about consensus, community was about care. We, too, were responsible for "the needs of the members." We didn't have to say "I agree with you." But we did, if we really wanted to go on being a community, need to be able to say, "I support your right and respect your need to do this."

By the time Ronald came to the community, some members from both sides of the community — those who wanted more change, those who wanted less — had been contemplating a split. I myself, as a member of the federation council, had received a petition from some of our own members to negotiate one. I remember standing backlit in a doorway, almost unable to see the face of the sister who delivered it, and saying into the darkness, "I believe that most splits do not do anything but destroy both groups. What will happen to those we leave behind? No, I will not do this." Then, I tore up the papers. These were not times simply of serious discussion. These were dark and dangerous times, times when people feared for their very lives, times when the very future of the community was at stake from pressures both outside and inside the group.

By the end of Ronald Fogarty's first meeting in Erie, in August 1969, the community had voted to allow all the major elements of constitutional change — veils, blouses, open placement, vacations, schedule changes, and personal budgets —

knowing that no one had to abide by any of them, knowing, too, that most of the community would.

The day after Ronald closed the workshop, Sister Carolyn Gorny-Kopkowski made final profession. "You're going to take the whole community with you to the altar on Sunday," she remembers being told. "I had been wrestling for days about whether I would wear the veil for the ceremony or not," she said. "Should I or shouldn't I? What would be best for the community?" By the end of the workshop, she recalls, she knew what to do. "First I thought, no, I won't. Then I said to myself, "We're walking together into the future and the future is going to be different. And I didn't wear it."

But the real meaning of the event was not that Carolyn, young, new, only now out of formation, didn't wear the veil. The real symbol of the event was that Mary Margaret, on the altar with her as receiving prioress, didn't wear a veil either. Up in the gallery I remember that when Carolyn said her vows I repeated my own and unbeknownst to anyone around me, quietly slipped my ring from my right hand, where it had been put at the time of my profession in the Erie Benedictines as they were in 1957, to my left hand now, a sign of commitment to the Erie Benedictines born anew in this day and age. In fact, we were all beginning again. And Carolyn, an intuitive, spiritual, feeling kind of person, went on, "Walking down the aisle at the end of the ceremony, I felt a big shift."

The second major element in the healing of the renewal process was the opening of the new monastery itself. With the old building went old rules about space, old memories of another kind of life. In its place came a new way of being women together in large beautiful spaces and private rooms and on great open grounds.

With it, too, came a new way of receiving guests. We began to bring visitors into the community dining room itself to serve them coffee, to give them lunch, rather than serve them on tiny silver trays in small, stiff, private parlors.

There was a new way of keeping silence in the new building as well. With the residence halls separate from the gathering spaces in the monastery, rather than times of silence, the community gravitated toward a respect for places of silence. Now sisters could rest, read, and study in their bedrooms without interruption and still find someone to talk to in other parts of the houses when they came home now that everyone no longer worked or slept in the same places.

The building of the Mount, once a financial threat to our existence, now, ironically, gave us the very space we needed to begin to exist differently.

Finally, perhaps the most telling moment of all in the history of reconciliation came out of tragedy. Here death became life before our very eyes. In 1971, Sisters Mary Bernard Niebling and Ellen Niebling, along with their parents, were killed in an automobile accident in Michigan.

The Niebling family had intended to surprise the son, in whose wedding they had all had a part twenty-five years before, by being present for the vow renewal ceremony that was scheduled for the next morning. Both sisters were artists. Sister Mary Bernard was forty-two years old; Ellen was thirty-five. Mary Bernard wore a modified habit; Ellen was in contemporary clothes. If any two people were universally loved by the community, if any two people so embodied both poles of the community theology, these two did.

The four long caskets were strung out along the wall in the large front reception room of the Mount. Community members stood in stunned silence while people poured into the Mount from the city. Both sisters were respected; both sisters had left their mark on very different kinds of people. All of a sudden the whole process of social change became very clear. It wasn't the dress or the work or the theology that mattered here. It was the people, their lives, the witness of goodness and kindness and whole-hearted giving of self that mattered. The community that had come so close to disintegrating, in this moment when the essentials of life, of community, were laid bare for the world to see, found one another again.

Sixteen sisters, some in veils, some not, donned white gloves, and, with eight on each casket, for the first time in

the history of the community, with the entire community behind them, carried their own to the grave. Their own, like
themselves, were different but alike, alike but different. And
in those differences, they sensed, lay their real unity. At the
door of the packed church, people saw the sight and a ripple
went across the congregation. No one doubted, neither the sisters nor the people, that the Erie Benedictines, whatever their
differences, however much they seemed to have changed, had
really not changed at all. This was a community, the kind not
bound by conformity to rigid regulations but by unity of heart,
by unity in lifestyle, by unity in commitment to one another.

The sudden confluence of factors — organizational, physical, emotional, and psychological — changed the direction of
the group from hopeless division to a common hope that just
as, over the years, the community had survived epidemics
of tuberculosis and influenza, poverty and near economic
collapse, they would survive change together too.

Renewal was far from over, maybe at heart not even begun,
but the horizontal violence in the group itself had ended and
the real work of change could now begin.

Through it all, Mary Margaret had been buffeted between
the poles of religious life, from one side to the other, from one
need to the next.

Part Four

Revitalization

I'm not sure that the community knew when, at what moment, we stepped out of "renewal" into revitalization. But there is a difference in the two phases. "Renewal" concentrates on what has to be changed. Revitalization changes it.

Someplace along the line we stopped talking about "what we needed to change next." Instead, we began to question what we were doing now.

The difference between the two postures is monumental. One concentrates on breaking out of an old cocoon. The other one owns being the butterfly, being something new, being something that is ready to fly.

Someplace along the line we got restless and wanted to fly again. Together.

Our lifestyle had changed. We thought of ourselves as adults now. We were treating one another as adults now. Our public presence had changed. We weren't invisible anymore. We weren't anonymous, interchangeable parts anymore. We were individual people who had chosen to live a life of prayer, service, and community as followers of Jesus. Our sense of self had changed. Each of us had a gift, a talent, a mission, and an obligation to use those personal qualities for others, for the coming of the reign of God. We had, indeed, grown up. I sat behind the community every day, feeling the restlessness, knowing that we were on the way but nowhere yet. My question became the *mantra that plagued me: Now that we had grown up, what did we grow up for? And how would we find out?*

The shift from one worldview to another and the development of new confidence and commitment in people, as imperative as those processes are to navigating the shoals of life, nevertheless do not guarantee the success of a social transition. Transition requires not only that a group leave one way of being in the world but that it manage to find another, just as important, just as satisfying, just as impacting.

We needed two things, I felt. First, we needed a total commitment to newness. Second, we needed an equally impelling commitment to maintaining the sense of purpose that had fired our successful past. It was not going to be automatic, this transition from personal development to revitalization. It would take great energy. The question was, Did we have it?

I could hear the murmurs: "There are too many people in the house," some said, still certain that monasteries were off limits to everyone but us. "There are too many things going on," others said, still more inclined to equate monasticism with routine than with presence. "There are too few of us to start so many things," a few said, still steeped in past notions that someone would be needed to replace the people who started these new activities someday. The concerns were real, authentic, necessary to the balance that Benedictinism is meant to bring. But the concerns were not the major concerns of the day if this Benedictine monastery was ever to be new again.

Revitalization requires more than papering over the past, repainting the system, resuscitating what is noble but dwindling. Revitalization means giving old inspiration to new ideas. It means beginning new directions for the same reason we began the old ones. And with the same vigor.

It was the vigor that was the question. Once comfort sets in, complacency is never far behind. We had come part of the way already. Could we, would we, go all the way?

What longevity of tradition does not motivate religious orders, or any long-established institution, to realize is that death is as much a part of institutional life as it is of organic life. When *a system wears out, when it ceases as it is to have meaning to the society in which it exists, when it fails to relate to the world around it in newly meaningful and life-giving ways, when the work necessary to one generation ends, systems either change or die.*

The world has seen many groups, vital at one time, that ceased to exist at another. The Pony Express ended with the railroad. The Erie Canal disappeared when the highway system emerged. Single sex clubs and schools ceased to be common coinage with the rise of the women's movement. But that is not defeat. To have a system die at the top of its history may be the most complimentary thing that can be said about it. It succeeded. There was nothing more the system could do in the society it was in — except begin again to serve a new one in a new way.

It's the courage and the vision of beginning again that is the essence of revitalization.

The problem with revitalization is that it depends on the very generation that brought the past to fullness to bring a new generation, a new endeavor to life. It asks those whose whole lives had been subsumed by what has just begun to seem eternal, unending, perfect to begin all over again, in the dark, without a clear goal, with little or no end in sight to create what the world needs now. But who knows exactly what it is.

Revitalization is a try-and-fail world. It demands vision, it demands trust, it demands the reckless release of talent, it demands creativity, and it demands faith in a future no one can see. That's the task we were now to be about.

Revitalization is no task for the timid.

20

When Community Is Not Enough

VATICAN II MANDATED the renewal of religious life. It also spelled out the criteria by which to judge it. But ordering a group to renew and making it happen are two different things. The question ate away now at the center of every thinking woman's soul: Was it really possible?

Religious around the world were instructed to do three things.

First, they were to determine whether or not they were still living "the charism of the founder." Were they still filled with the same fire, devoted to the same ends for which they had been founded? Anything in the way of that, the document said, could now be eliminated. Whatever the legislation, ecclesiastical or internal, that had accrued from past eras to damp the fire could be considered annulled.

Many communities discovered that somewhere along the line, the charism had been hijacked. Orders founded to work with the poorest of the poor had wound up serving only the richest of the rich. Many of them, founded to work with street people, had at least a kind of quasi-cloister foisted upon them to accord with the public standard imposed on women everywhere. Others, like the Erie Benedictines, who said that their charism was "to seek God in community and to respond in prayer and ministry" realized that as the proverb so aptly described it, the cart had been put before the horse. Teaching had simply consumed them to the point where community had been diminished to routine and prayer was more formulaic than reflective.

But Erie and I had another problem: we were almost fifteen hundred years away from "the intention of the founder." Where did we go to discover what fire drove Benedict of Nursia in 480 CE out of a hermit's cave in Italy to respond to the shepherds of the area who were seeking his spiritual direction? What was it that drove him to develop a community lifestyle saying that they were "the most valiant kind of monks," in a world full of hermit monks, wandering monks, and public preacher types?

I was convinced that to take any particular period of monastic history, short of the Rule itself, as a template for renewal had to be a mistake. I resolved that the Rule, not Benedictine "history," mottled as it was from one century to another, one country to another over time, had to be bedrock for me. Anything else simply flirted with trying more to revive a period than a charism.

Second, they were to consider "the needs of the members." What most people fail to realize is that membership had already begun to decline before Vatican II even began. For the first time in history, people were coming to religious life — and leaving it. Perpetually professed or not. Was it because religious life had become irreligious in its religious fervor? Was it oppressing people more than freeing them for joyous lives in the service of God on earth? What human needs did religious life itself make impossible to meet?

In Erie, I knew that before renewal "the needs of the members" had been long ignored. As young novices walking in the convent yard at night, we looked up at the rickety fourth floor porch, where the older sisters sat and rocked, silent and dour, stone-faced and cross, night after night, and made one another promise never to allow any of us to get like that. Why were they like that, we wondered? Clearly, something happened to people here as life went by that sapped their energies and smothered their spirits. Only after Mary Margaret lifted the restrictions, opened the doors of the house, encouraged people to come and go, listened to them, gave parties for them, did we see the older sisters begin to laugh and live again.

With new concern for the real needs of the members, the tenor of the community changed.

Third, religious were to examine whether or not they were in tune with "the signs of the times." Did we even know what they were? Had we determined how, in the light of our own initial purpose, we could meet those now? Were religious doing what people needed at the present time or were we simply doing what we insisted people needed? Were we doing what people were looking for now or were we simply repeating what had met the needs of generations before us and so continued them over and over again?

By the time I became prioress in 1978, two of the three Vatican mandates to religious were already well in process.

Sister Alice had contended with "the charism of the founder" and found that the way we had been attempting to live it was, at best, wanting.

The role and place of women had changed in the twentieth century, light years away from its nineteenth-century German agricultural roots. A growing number of new poor within two blocks of the inner-city monastery needed help just as badly as the German immigrants whom the community had first served in that same area. But trapped on our property, absorbed by our schools, dependent on parish salaries, we were powerless to do a thing about it.

The rise of an educated population had changed the very nature of life in the United States and so made new professional demands on religious as well. But what were they? And if that weren't confusing enough, a new generation of theologians and liturgists was even beginning to imagine change in the church itself.

Alice had tried to make adjustments in the character of religious life to keep pace with such an increasingly urban and industrialized culture. She wanted the community to be able to pray in English so that prayer could become a more personal,

contemplative experience for this active but contemplative tradition. She set out to raise the cultural level of a community
made up almost entirely of women from working class families. She wanted to develop strong professional women rather
than a community of docile girls. She wanted to open the community to the world around it by lifting the cloister regulations
left over from the medieval cloistering European monasteries of
nuns, at least to allow sisters to visit their own family homes.

In retrospect, the moves were basically simple ones, but they
struck at the root of the question of "charism," of the real
purpose of religious life. Was religious life simply an exercise
in personal asceticism? Or was it for the sake of the world
around it — as it had been at its founding when Benedict left
the cave at Subiaco to catechize the shepherds. As it was during
the Middle Ages when monasteries were the flywheels of an
agrarian society. As it was until canonical regulations after the
Council of Trent and the church's reaction to the Protestant
Reformation introduced more rigidity than theological reform.

Mary Margaret, caught in the cross-fire between Vatican I's
negative regard for the world and Vatican II's openness to
the world, spent her entire administration struggling primarily
with "the needs of the members." They needed new theological development. They needed personal development. They
needed cultural adaptation. They needed to sift through the
sands of their lives from the beginning. They needed to start
over again, in heart, in mind, and in soul.

The hard work of internal renewal had been accomplished
by the time I became prioress, but I never for a moment
doubted the meaning or the urgency of the third criterion of
renewal, the need to determine the signs of the times.

All our lives we had taught together, lived together, prayed
together, and worked together. Now, good as it was to encourage human development and support a sister's search for a
personal ministry, we were, at the same time, becoming fragmented. I sat in counseling sessions for hours with people,
heard the anomie in them, felt their discouragement, listened
while women who had never questioned their vocation now

suddenly wondered aloud if it wouldn't be better for them to leave. They had no reason, no place to go. They simply didn't have much of a reason to stay anymore.

Night after night, I wrestled with the problem. People, I knew, joined groups only in order to do together what they could not do alone. What were we doing together that we could not do alone? Prayer? Hardly. Community life? Not if marriage and family still counted. Work? Not anymore.

It's hard for me to know exactly what was going on in the mind of the community when I became prioress. I can't tell the story now from that side of the desk with the same surety with which I could explain the undercurrents of the administrations before me. After all, in those eras, I had lived in the mainstream of a process that shook the timbers of the house. But I know without doubt what was going on in me in 1978 and why I made the choices I did in my own administration.

For seven years, as president of the federation and president of the Leadership Conference of Women Religious, I had watched community after community in the country floundering around issues of ministry. Some of them tried desperately to save the colleges and schools and hospitals that came out of their origins or capped their success in the eras before them. Others watched them decline one by one — for reasons of population, for reasons of money, for reasons of professional limitations — but had not a clue which way to go next.

Like everyone else around me, I had been changed by the process of renewal. I had come to realize that I valued the community, as community, more than I valued any single custom, any particular practice. Those things could go, I decided, as long as something worth being, worth doing, emerged in their place. I wanted religious life, not medieval life. I hadn't made changes in my life because I no longer believed in religious life. On the contrary. It was simply that I no longer believed that religious life as we had lived it had the magnetism or the meaning to move a modern culture. Women may have liked us but they were not joining us. There was clearly a disconnect somewhere.

I definitely believed that religious life had a role to play in the church and in society. But it had to be in this church and this society, not in a church or society long gone culturally and now even officially. I also believed that, although we had had a clear place before Vatican II as teachers of an immigrant church, our new role in a new age was now dangerously unclear.

The nineteenth-century Catholic community had integrated into Protestant society. They no longer needed to be self-consciously or politically Catholic, nor did they intend to maintain the Catholic enclaves that had nurtured and protected that kind of denominational character in them. Even Catholic social clubs — the Polish Falcons, the Italian Nuova Aurora, the German Turners — all remnants of past and primary ethnic identities, were disbanding. Catholics had become "American," just like the immigrants before them.

Furthermore, teaching itself, once the main service of most religious communities in a world where education was more a luxury than a public utility, had become mainstream. The state educational system was now both compulsory and comfortably pluralistic. At the same time, Catholic schools were disappearing under the strain of high costs, fewer sister-teachers, and declining enrollments.

Obviously one particular brand of religious life — clearly vital at one time but approaching the abstruse in a democratic and technological world — no longer had either the dynamism or the social seedbed that had marked its American beginnings. In an earlier era whole Catholic communities grew up around the newly founded monasteries and convents everywhere. At the same time religious orders followed Catholic emigrants to the United States and settled among them, in large cities, on the Great Plains, in rural areas beyond reach of public services. They opened schools and hospitals and orphanages in these places. Its poorest and least wanted citizenry, Catholics, instead of sinking into bottomless ethnic and denominational ghettoes, poor and destitute and ignorant, rose rapidly in the new society. They learned the language from the sisters. They learned business skills from the sisters. They kept the faith, in large part because of the catechetical efforts of the sisters. Catholicism thrived, as a result, despite the then Protestant bias of the country. And the religious communities that served them thrived too. Ethnic seedbeds produced one generation after another of women religious whose families nurtured the thought of vocation and whose society had little place for women outside the home except the convent. But those days were now long gone. The Catholic ghettoes were now gone. The Catholic enclaves were gone. The Catholics themselves were gone, melted into an amorphous society, not of immigrants, but of "Americans."

I knew just as certainly that even another form of religious life, however "updated," would either disappear entirely or deteriorate quickly into a kind of cultic mystique if it lacked clear purpose for its existence.

Whatever my analysis of the situation then — perhaps precisely because of that analysis — I had no desire to be prioress. In the first place, I had already been First Councilor to Mary Margaret for almost fourteen years. I had lived through the polarization, the pressures, the uncertain changes. I knew first hand that the road ahead would be more difficult than anyone now realized if we were ever to become a vibrant community again. In the second place, I knew, it was one thing to take a community down into the tomb of "renewal." It was another thing entirely to resurrect it again. In this case, it would be even harder than usual.

Resources were low. The mortgage on the new Mount still hung decisively over our heads. This was no time for great new debt. My experience as president of the Leadership Conference of Women Religious gave me an overview of a religious life that extended far beyond the boundaries even of Benedictinism, let alone the Erie Benedictines. Most other groups of women religious were large and vast and centralized and rich in resources, both physical and personal. We were not.

In an era when religious congregations commonly included thousands of members, there were only 138 of us. Community cohesion, come unmoored by the ideological tensions of the past ten years, though healed of downright hostility now, was nevertheless still at an all-time low. We liked one another but who we were together now, as a group, as a community, was anybody's guess. Confusion reigned. And I knew it.

What's more, I came into the election after only two of three possible terms as president of the federation. Being the idea agent and a kind of roving ombudsman for the twenty-three member monasteries of the group was a position that seemed to suit me. In my mind, I would finish a third term in the federation at the age of forty-six and return to some kind of ministry with time enough left to enable me finally to build a professional life of my own.

In fact, life for me had already been interrupted once before this. The very week I defended my doctoral dissertation in 1971 for the first doctoral degree in the history of the community, I became federation president. Life had been on hold ever since. This time, I was sure, would be different.

By the time the community election was over, though, the new degree in communication theory with its emphasis on social psychology and organizational communications, had fizzled in midair. By accepting the election as prioress rather than seeking an academic appointment, I would now never get a chance to use that material, it seemed. Nothing could have been more wrong.

Several months ago I found a small piece of paper tucked into my novitiate copy of the Rule. I hadn't seen it for years. It was dated June 21, 1978. It said it all.

As the community sat in chapel that day, the public reading of the votes for prioress got stronger and stronger. I had obviously scribbled down some ideas to guide my remarks when, it was clear, the presider would call me to the altar to announce the results of the election. I had taken it with me to the microphone that day. I remember saying those words quite clearly. The little piece of scrap paper read: "Sister Mary Margaret Kraus enabled this community to grow up. Now we have to ask ourselves what we grew up for."

On that day, at that moment, we began together consciously and as a community to determine "the signs of the
times" and their meaning to the real renewal of contemporary
religious life.

I began what became an era of new community initiatives.
Going back, I knew, was impossible because, if nothing else,
there was nothing and nowhere to go back to. What had sus-
tained us, identified us, secured us for our first hundred years
was gone now. Going ahead was the only possible direction left
to take if we wanted to exist.

As a result, the time was marked by risk, by daring. We did
together what no group in debt, in decline, in confusion, it
might seem, should have done. And it was exactly the right
thing to do.

I knew deep down in my heart that religious life as we had
known it, however much we had lived it well, was dead. "The
only question now," I was fond of saying to religious, was,
"What do we want to be caught dead doing?" I, for one, wanted
to die following Jesus the contemplative — the contemplative
Jesus — from Galilee to Jerusalem doing good: healing the sick,
raising the dead, contending with the legalists' interpretation of
the Law, empowering women as he did the Samaritan woman
to "go into the town and tell them who and what you have
seen. . . . And on whose account thousands believed that day."

We launched a season of new beginnings at what, to many,
may well have seemed to be a dizzying, maybe even a reckless,
pace. If Jesus and the gospel were really the model as the Rule
implied, then, long consumed by internal agendas and Catholic works while the world and its poor changed right around
our heads, we had some catching up to do. Women, the world,
and the planet were waiting for us. We had no time to wait.
The times were rife with new issues. The groans of a world
in search of justice could be heard in the streets. This was no
time to preside over a monastic museum, to dig moats around
monasteries while they took the poor to the jails and the flop
houses and the Salvation Army at night but never thought of

asking for help at a convent whose order, we were proud to say, had "saved European civilization."

I spent twelve years continuing to support individual development and services but beginning, as well, to develop the notion of the community as a public person, a ministering person, a prophetic person in its own right.

When I entered the community, community itself, in some vague and bloodless way, subsumed and superseded the person. Now, we were on the brink of watching the persons supersede the community. We were a collection of individuals living with good people and doing good works but what was the community itself about? Why were we together? What were any of us doing there?

Those questions consumed me. And, I realized, there was an important place for them on the monastery level just as there had been at the level of the federation. Why do this? Why not do that? Why, why, why became a mantra for me, and I set out to pursue the answer. Living with nice people who prayed regularly was. . . . well, nice. But, something told me, it was not enough if, as the Vatican documents said, religious really were "the prophetic dimension of the church" and "religious life had a role to play in the development of the times."

The truth was that Benedictine history itself gave proof of the long-lived effect of Benedictine monasteries on the society around it. In this sterile, materialistic world in which we lived, up to our hearts in nuclear weapons, rich at the expense of others, and lacking the voices and values of women, religious life was not unnecessary, irrelevant, outdated. It was simply out of touch with itself.

Our monasteries, I was convinced, needed to become havens for the weary, signs of hope to the hopeless, centers of spiritual development for all.

But what was the way forward? By what method? And, most of all, with what effect on all our lives?

21

Cherishing the Past, Accepting the Future

W HEN I BECAME PRIORESS in June 1978, there was one
scripture passage that strummed like a descant in my
soul. Its refrain hung like a specter over every decision, every
question, every moment of my life. "O Lord," I prayed over and
over again, "can these bones live again?" (Ezek. 37:1–14)

Somehow, like dazed bystanders on the edge of a volcano we
had managed to stay together through years in which separation seemed the only possible solution to the depths of the
ideological division that marked the community after Vatican II. But here we were, still clinging to hope, still moving
toward a future that had no shape, still intent on saving what
may well have been long dead. Somehow or other we had
managed, apparently, to close the circle again. But could it last?

I remember standing in chapel some days before the election
of 1978, heavy-hearted over the change in my own life that I
could almost feel in the air. Being president of the federation
had been like watching the evolution of religious life in microcosm, under glass. Prioresses, on the other hand, were dealing
with renewal up close and personal. Too close and too personal. No doubt about it, being president was one thing, but
prioress? I had my doubts. The thought of the interpersonal
work tempted me because I liked people; the thought of the
organizational challenges were, to put it mildly, sobering.

My questions were real ones as I looked out over the community in chapel that morning: Did we have the human

172

resources it would take for real renewal? We were by national standards a very small group. Did we have enough emotional energy left, after the war of ideas we'd just come through, to do what would really need to be done if we were to have new meaning in a new world? Did we have the finances it would take to sponsor new activities as well as sustain the ones we already had? St. Benedict Academy was on the brink of financial failure monthly. Schools were closing everywhere, and work was not easy to find. The mortgage on the new building was still huge. Almost half the group was over fifty. Was it faith — or foolishness — to think that anything could possibly be done now and here? And how much help could we possibly get in the doing of it from a public, some of whom were angry about our changes, most of whom were confused by them? Had it all been wrong in the first place?

Why large groups of women religious, the Erie Benedictines among them, made such apparently radical changes in lifestyle in so short a period of time has never been subjected to rigorous psychological research. But there are pieces of data along the way that give a fair picture of the situation. *Climb along the Cutting Edge: An Analysis of Change in Religious Life*[8] traces the history of the process at the federation level. It explores the pre–Vatican II lifestyle of the member communities, the theology of the vows basic to the formation of women religious prior to Vatican II, and the process employed by the federation to launch and monitor experimentation throughout the member houses. Most important of all, perhaps, it records the responses of those federation delegates to the changes initiated by the renewal chapters. It explores renewal from on high, in other words. It gives a picture of corporate engineering. It does not explore, however, the effect of that engineering on the sisters themselves. The theory of change and the experience of change are not the same thing.

Inside each community, on the other hand, there was another dynamic in the renewal of religious life that went beyond the history of ideas. In addition to decisions made by either church or federation officials to allow experimentation in religious orders, the factor of group living itself exerted major influence on a group's state and pace of change.

Prior to Vatican II and its mandate to make religious life relevant to the needs and times of the present century, religious communities by and large had been "total institutions," some more than others. A sister's entire life was spent inside the group. The religious community was, in fact, an ecosystem of its own. Members were formed there, worked there, lived there, socialized there, and died there. One generation passed on to the next its structures, expectations, customs, and processes. Contact with the outside world existed but only erratically and only in limited ways. It was a closed information system. But without new information, new thinking, new contacts, the hope for new creativity grew slimmer and slimmer as the years went by.

No wonder then that tradition — meaning "our routines" — had become such a major factor in the group lifestyle. When I entered the Erie Benedictines, for instance, the layout of the community wardrobe and kitchen, the public rooms and storage areas, the guest parlors and priest's dining room, had not changed for generations. Everything had a place; the same place it had had for decades. Everything had a way. Novices were taught how to hold a dust cloth in one hand, an oil cloth in the other and to apply each with a circular motion in opposite directions when dusting the pews in chapel. Otherwise, you learned quickly, the pews had not been done "correctly." The cracks between the hall floorboards were cleaned out with "city chicken sticks," pointed wooden skewers, or the halls couldn't possibly be clean. No one even dared suggest getting vacuum cleaners or rugs or tile. "We've always done it this way" and "the Hail Mary never changes" were community jests — but not terribly funny ones. They carried a message of deep and fundamental meaning: We do things this way. We think this about that. We don't do such things. There is only one right way to do this and this is it. Time had stopped. Thinking had stopped. Life had stopped. No wonder, then, that ideas rarely changed.

Without doubt, total institutions do not change easily. So how can we explain such a major shift in so large a group in so short a time?

Not until the twentieth century did anyone even try to investigate such a question. What we know now about how groups function may go far to explain why the renewal of religious communities — whose very hallmark had been changelessness, permanence, inflexibility — swept across the country like fire in high grass.

Scholars tell us that the presence of others is likely to affect us in three ways. First, when others are present we respond more frequently and more quickly to a situation. Second, when others are present we are likely to be less accurate but more productive. Third, when others are present we are more concerned with what others around us in the group are thinking than we are when we are alone. And furthermore, just to know that others are working on the same questions somewhere else has the same effect as if they were with us as we work.[9]

But religious, by definition, were always together. What one religious, one community thought, asked, began, believed in became infectious. Renewal was not a personal, private activity. It was the activity of religious with religious.

Unlike priests, who for the most part lived alone during Vatican II and the renewal period that followed it, or laypeople, whose family lives insulated them from the thinking or activities of their peers, religious lived in groups where psychological bonds were strong, where both the pressure to respond and the pressure to conform were high, and where groups of religious everywhere were dealing with the same material.

Groupness itself, then, the fact of belongingness, association, and emotional bonding as well as intellectual or theoretical identification with the tradition, was a factor in renewal.[10] We talked about renewal, its problems and possibilities, day and night. We listened for word of what other groups were doing as a result of it with an eagerness that bordered on compulsion. We found ourselves wrestling first with the arguments from one part of the community, then with the dreams of the other. These were people who had committed themselves to the same things, were one another's full support and shared all the important moments of life together. What the other members of the community thought, wanted, feared was not just "interesting." It was the very lifeblood of the group.

Most rudimentary of all, perhaps, we cared about one another as people. Many of us had been friends since grade school. We saw one another as models. Ours, after all, was a woman's world led by women. We took women leaders for granted. We were accustomed to learning from one another. We were all in this together.

What happened to part of us happened to all of us and, worse, we were all we had. We were ripe for group decision-making. What we decided for ourselves, we were deciding not only for the rest of the group but with the rest of the group. We were confederates in the success — or in failure — of our common goals. We had to be united, in other words, to be able to be ourselves. Our own interests, each of us knew — spiritual, professional, personal — all depended on the success of the group. This was no time to fracture it. We were living together in the middle of a snowball that was rolling downhill. There was no way to stop the process, hardly any way to slow it. We would either decide how to live newly or die together.

What's more, the Erie Benedictines shared the heritage of an order that was almost fifteen hundred years old. In this case, perhaps, the tradition carried us as much or more as we carried the tradition. However uncertain we ourselves may have felt in the midst of it all, one thing we knew for sure: Benedictinism had been through all of this before and survived. Benedictinism had survived the fall of the Roman empire, feudalism, the rise of national states, the bubonic plague, popes and antipopes, the division of Christendom, and two world wars. Not to worry, then. We had made it before; even stumbling, we would make it again. Confidence was built right into the system.

The Erie Benedictines, like religious congregations across the country, knew in their own bones, out of their own lives, that renewal was necessary. What's more, women religious everywhere were wrestling with the need to reshape religious life itself. Finally, they knew that life as they had known and lived it stood daily more rejected by this new world around them. They all knew after years of membership losses that theological speculation was not what they were really about. Their very survival depended on their ability to bring religious life into the twentieth century.

They knew, too, though people on each side of the community divide had flirted with the idea of simply dividing the community along ideological lines, that real success depended on their being able to negotiate the shoals of renewal together. Religious had simply done too much together along the way — raised great hospitals, opened scores of orphanages, built a whole school system, missionized whole societies — to ignore the innate potential of community life. They liked each other as people too much to simply walk out on one another, on the elderly who had raised them — many of them in their schools as well as in the community — on the women with whom they had grown up.

They believed in religious life or they too would have left it years ago. Renewal was not an excuse for abandoning religious life. On the contrary. Renewal marked the way to make what had been life-giving for many just as life-giving for a whole new generation, a whole new culture. But what was this religious life they loved without the others who had made it real for them? In Erie, as in so many other communities, they knew that they wanted to do it together.

Doing things together, however, is exactly where renewal became as much an exercise in organizational development as it was in spiritual development. What they may not have known is that both the lure and the wisdom of doing things together lies in the fact that groups are far more inclined to level one another's ideas than they are either to ratchet them up or to suppress them. The implications of those findings should give a group pause: in the process of group renewal, both ends of the ideogram are prone to be rejected. Neither the most creative ideas nor the most reactionary are likely to be honored.[11] One major implication is, of course, that extremists need not apply. The other is that neither rigid conservatism nor maximum liberalism normally prevail in established groups. Neither unremitting traditionalism nor utmost creativity promise to triumph. So, though renewal depended on their being renewed together, the questions for many were still how little and how much?

In addition to Erie's own internal concerns, religious everywhere were also being affected now by the expectations of other groups: the laypeople with whom they were beginning to work more closely, the clergy in whose programs or parishes most of them were employed, the church and its new theological principles, their families, and their own traditional expectations or, in many cases, their long-suppressed concerns about the repressive nature of convent life. Even the changing attitudes of students had relevance for them. "I remember very distinctly," one young sister said, "watching priests remove their clerical collars, pull on sweaters, and pile the kids in their cars after school to take them for hamburgers. No wonder they liked the priests and avoided the sisters. All they saw of us after school was when we kept them for detention."

The changes came, in other words, but it was not always easy to tell why. Was it for theological reasons or was it because of social pressure? And, frankly, did it make any difference in the long run which reason predominated as long as the necessary changes were finally made? The question is more than academic. It has something to do with whether or not change would be internalized or simply experienced. It had something to do with permanence. Was renewal a house built upon rock — or upon sand? Would it last?

In the early stages of renewal, there was at least as much compliance as there was conformity to the new process. Conformity, according to traditional definitions, is "a change of belief or behavior as a result of real or imagined group pressure."[12] Conformity implies that, however distinct their starting points, their backgrounds, their initial beliefs or behaviors, the members of a group become more alike than different as time goes by. Their goals become more united, their behaviors and reactions more comparable, their likes and dislikes more similar with each conversation and group discussion.

The more a person believes in the group, the more a person becomes like the other members of a group in what they think and believe and do. "If the community is not going to wear a veil," one sister told me, "I'm not going to wear a veil either, much as I would prefer to have one. We're a community and we should be doing this together." She abandoned a cherished behavior because she believed in a present form of community witness more than she believed in maintaining an individual preference for past policies. She believed in what the group believed. She conformed her mind to the mind of the group. Compliance, on the other hand, deals with behavior only, not with belief. The compliant do what the rest of the group does but the way they feel about it or what they really believe at base about what they're doing is never at issue. They "go along" or they "cooperate" or they tolerate. They do a thing to be liked, perhaps, or to maintain what they see as a necessary relationship to the group or to be socially correct. In a situation where the very leaders of the group itself — federation leaders, community leaders, or chapter delegates — approved of experimentation, compliance became almost imperative, even when understanding or emotional acceptance lagged. But that does not mean that compliance is either unreal or ineffective. On the contrary.

In many instances, in fact, attitude change follows behavior change rather than precedes it. "I never believed that we could allow people in the community dining room and still be a community," a sister said. "Now I see that taking others in really means that we can all be together instead of having to go out to meet friends and co-workers for dinner elsewhere." The case spoke clearly to the theory. I come to believe in what I'm doing because I see what it can do — even though I never foresaw its value at first blush. I try a thing before I pronounce judgment on it. Indeed, compliance is not to be disregarded as an important dimension of social change. In fact, it may be exactly what makes a more objective evaluation of a program possible at a later time.

In the course of renewal, some sisters conformed; some complied. For some renewal was a dream; for others it was a test.

There were advantages and disadvantages, strengths and weaknesses, spiritual depth and spiritual fancy to renewal. The testing of each depended as much on experience as it did on theory. Renewal was made up of two kinds of people: "true believers," those who were privately committed to its ideology, and "followers," those who acceded to the changes for reasons other than their acceptance of the new theology. Some people simply accepted change for the sake of the welfare of the group itself. But that was all the group needed to try out the theories meant to take an ancient lifestyle and make it new without, at the same time, making it "relevant" but vacuous. One approach became the prod of the other. Without the counterpoints of conformity and compliance to test the theoretical theology, renewal could easily have become superficial, inane, meaningless. Instead, theory prodded practice and practice corrected the theory.

As a result, the advantages and the disadvantages of renewal became plain for all to see and with them a sense of future direction that would guide the community for the next twelve years.

22

Giving Context to Change

THERE IS NO SUCH THING, social scientists know now, as "controlled change." Change is a dynamic that builds a coherent future out of a chaotic present. Change, if it is real, takes us where we have not been before and could never have imagined that we'd go. It takes the courage of an explorer, the fancy of a dreamer. The process is simple: there is either control or change. You can't have it both ways.

Mary Margaret had begun a change process. Like Pope John XXIII, she brought speakers in from across the country to "open the windows" of religious life, trusting that if what we were doing was done for the right motives, was really "religious," it would, in the end, all come out right. As a result, the community had high energy for the task. Anything was possible. But nobody knew exactly what it was we were to do. Or, worse, why we ought to do it.

It was up to me, I decided, to bring some kind of meaning to Benedictinism itself again, to link it to the tradition that could give it roots, make it firm, allow it to grow. Just exactly what did it mean to be "Benedictine" now and here? In fact, did it mean anything at all anymore? Most of all, what did it mean to our own small community in one small town that knew very little about who we were and what we were doing?

After having done doctoral study in social psychology and then, as president of the federation, studies in monastic theology and history, I decided to do what I did best: I decided to take time to think the whole process through again. This time, though, we would do it together and this time not for the sake of "changing" anything. We would do it just for the sake of understanding where we'd come from, who we were, and what was happening to us. So I began a series of monthly lectures in the community that were totally unrelated to any specific "recommendations" or impending "resolutions" or adventuresome activities. No decisions were required at the end of any of them, just talk, just discussion of the ideas they provoked in our own lives. These were not presentations meant to "sell" anything, as most of the renewal position papers were meant to do and so led many to view them with caution, if not mistrust. After these presentations we could all just sit back and think.

I remember the first conference very well. It took place in chapel on a "First Sunday" or traditional community reflection day. Long before I entered, the first Sunday of every month had been kept as a regular retreat day. On "First Sundays" the community kept silence, had Adoration of the Blessed Sacrament, and, usually, a conference. On this First Sunday, to their surprise, I'm sure, I got out of my pew during the community's holy hour and walked up to the ambo. I would, I said, hardly daring to look at them, be giving monthly conferences — something that had traditionally been done by the priest celebrant but never by a prioress. It was a step in claiming our womanhood, our education, our experience, and our right to explore and shape our own part of a Benedictine heritage. But it was a very small step. The conference took twenty minutes. Months later, as the process unfolded into Sunday afternoon discussions, someone asked me why the first one had been so short. "Because," I said, "then I was only trying out my knees, not my knowledge."

The purpose of this material was simply to broaden the backdrop for community decision-making in the future, to level the playing field between those younger people who were closer to formal study than many of the older members of the community, to provide a common universe of discourse, common language and filters and history through which we could consider both our new questions and our old answers.

Each lecture series was geared to create the theoretical context which, it seemed to me, the community would need in order to deal well with the issues to come, all of them at least as serious as the ones we'd already dealt with. Now we needed to look again at community life, community development, interpersonal relationships, community decision-making, spirituality, and ministry.

After years as a history teacher, I began to reteach the Rule of Benedict — which for many was the very reason it seemed that we should change nothing at all — with an eye to distinguishing between its values and the social system of the time in which they were embedded. The spiritual document of the Rule and the customs of the time that were meant to reflect them were two different things that over time had often become hopelessly conflated. Only a community that knew the difference between the two types of material in the Rule could really decide with ease which structures or customs could go and which must stay.

Then I taught Benedictine history. Just being able to discover that Benedictinism had always been lived variously, not uniformly, across all communities over all centuries, freed the group to think about its own history and possibilities.

Philosophers and theologians had long taught that women were emotionally unstable and intellectually incapable of study. Study had been kept for the men, the scholars, the rational beings of the order. Women got manual labor to subdue their passions and the practice of devotions. As a result, women had never been allowed to take courses in theology or monasticism, let alone matriculate for a degree. As a result, the secular world, not the church, took the lead in providing higher education for women. Women religious, as the foundresses of major colleges, hospitals, orphanages, and private academies across the country, concentrated on providing sisters with professional degrees in medicine, the arts, science, mathematics, history, literature, business, and sociology that would certify them to function in these arenas. It was these broader areas, therefore, that women brought to the questions of renewal and the role of religious in the modern world. The irony of the situation amuses me yet: it was precisely the women's lack of theological training and their proficiency in professional training that freed them to see the renewal of the church in a larger context than the men of the order who were concentrating almost entirely on its theological dimensions.

I myself was proof of the approach. I intended to present the Rule and the history of the order in its social context, to ask what Benedictinism had done for the world around it through the centuries and why, to study how the spiritual values of the Rule were demonstrated to the culture in which it was immersed, to measure how like, or unlike, the lifestyle of the monastery had been to the world around it. The Christology of the Rule was important, of course, but not as an artifact of an ancient document, only as a guide for living out that same Christ life now.

The Rule and Benedictine history ceased to be a weapon to be used against the autonomy of the community. Little by little, it became obvious, they were meant to be a guide to a good way of life here and now, not a straitjacket, not a quaint replica of an early age, not an obstacle to the gospel but the very ground of a gospel life today.

In another series of conferences, I taught my own major, communication theory. So much pain had been inflicted in the early days of renewal because communities, taught to keep silence, had never really been taught how to talk to one another. They knew how to work hard, but they did not know how to work ideas through without minimizing the ideas or the intentions of the other. As a result, otherwise good-hearted people knew little about how to avoid being sarcastic or demeaning or defensive or accusatory. Blundering speech, driven by fear, ate away at years of camaraderie. It eroded unity. It made both the common life and common purpose taut, fragile, emotionally impossible.

Then I drew from my background in psychology and taught human development to women, most of whom had entered at very early ages and were given hidebound rules rather than the value of experience as a guide to spiritual growth. Or worse, they were given the findings of male psychology that had been cavalierly applied to women, no proofs provided, no research designed to determine if what was good for men really was good for women or not. The awareness that as human beings we were all unfinished, all still growing, all able and fulfilled by change, all bearing the burdens and the blessings of our past erased the differences of age among us. It gave everyone the right to be wrong, to be unsure, to be honest about our own anxieties or insecurities in the face of change. The fact that we were women not men, other not less, strong not weak, and competent not inept as all current research everywhere attested gave substance to the independence, autonomy, and decision-making capabilities of women. We had, we began to realize together, both the gifts and the right to direct our own lives.

Then I opened a series on the history of spirituality in order to dispel the old notion that the pieties we had once practiced we had always to do. Spirituality and culture, I taught, were of a piece. It was practicing pieties that were proper to the time that counted. It was one thing to pray with outstretched arms in order to symbolize the cross, the material demonstrated. It was another thing to help the poor carry the crosses of their own lives. The fact is that religious life had been reduced almost entirely to symbol.

Finally, as social psychologist and communication theorist, I gave a series of lectures on organizational revitalization to indicate, just as the scriptures said of human death, there was such a thing as organizational death. But history also showed that the death did not need to be final. If we embraced revitalization rather than simply hoped for it, community life, like human life, at a time of social transition would not be "taken away but only changed." Refounding was possible. What was not possible was that it would happen by accident.

The message under all the lectures was essentially the same: as Newman had put it so well, "To live is to change; to be perfect is to have changed often."

Even the lectures themselves were not obligatory. I never took roll call. I never pronounced that everyone should be there. The announcement of the series simply said that on First Sundays of every month I would post a topic, and if any were interested in exploring it, they could come to the library and we'd talk about it together. The first presentation had been in chapel. After that they had to be held in the dining room because we couldn't fit in the library. Everybody came, regardless. There was no end to the interest. This was a community that wanted to make the world new again — starting with themselves. And they were not alone. This return to the roots of the life, to the beginning of new life for women, was happening in convents and monasteries everywhere.

This opening of areas of religious life that had been long hardened under the dried clay of time freshened whole aspects of the life. Instead of simply accepting longtime community traditions, women religious began to think all of them through again for value, meaning, application, depth. The lectures were just the beginning, the foundation, for what was in the air already and would affect virtually every facet of religious life, not simply in Erie, but in every congregation in the country. And what was in the air went far beyond the practice of "devotions" as the practice of the vows.

Personal Growth and Human Development

Personal development began to be seen as a conscious goal of religious life rather than an abandonment of the virtue of humility, as it had been defined. Taught for years not to look in mirrors, not to state their personal preferences, not to waste time on personal interests, sisters began to realize that applying their natural gifts to the needs of the time was as good for the people to whom they ministered as it was for themselves.

As a result, the horizons of religious life — and of the Benedictine Sisters of Erie — expanded beyond the confines of the Catholic culture. Nuns opened themselves to the whole world, to all its needs, to the entire human agenda as well as to Catholic causes.

Nuns were still nuns — still completely given to living a gospel life here and now, still vowed to spend themselves entirely for the coming of the reign of God, still committed to following the Word of God — but they changed their way of doing it. Still intent on selfless love, reckless generosity, openness to the will of God, they came to see those things as given for the sake of the whole human community, not simply for the sake of the Catholic population. More than that, rather than seeing themselves as some kind of anonymous and invisible pieces of a disembodied church, a sense of agency and personal responsibility emerged in them. Their faith matured. Spiritual dependents no longer, they became bearers of the tradition for themselves.

In Erie, sisters began to create retreat programs for other people. Laypeople began to "join" the community as oblates and associates either to concentrate on studying the spiritual tradition or to involve themselves with its ministries. Now the doors of the community were always open. The laity came for event after event. People began simply to "drop in." The monastery became more than a monastic residence. It became a center of life. The old intellectual drawbridges that had once separated us from the world around us came down and new energy began to flow through the halls.

The boundaries of life began to blur as religious not only went out to other parts of the world but began to take people into their own space as well. Were we different from other people or were we the same? And if we weren't different what were we?

It was a good time but it was a hard time too. The once sacrosanct confines of community space began to break down. People ate with us. People stayed overnight in the house with us. People were being brought right into our own infirmary for emergency care. Both women and men. The moment called for redefinition. What exactly was "community"? Was it separation from others or was it a family strong enough to remain itself even in the midst of others? A community that had lived for years engulfed in linens and scapulars, hidden behind convent doors and removed from public presence found itself face to face with swarms of people everywhere. In the chapel. In the guest rooms. In the dining room. In the community room. In the halls.

I heard the complaints over and over, remnants of a past life, signals of the creaking, groaning beginnings of a new one. Children had spilled things on the rugs, they told me — an obvious proof that children should not be allowed in the community room. Women had talked outside of chapel, a clear indicator that we could not possibly pray undisturbed anymore. Men were drinking coffee in the dining room. How could sisters go there in the morning for coffee before prayer? But there was no single answer now that worked hard and fast for everyone at every time. To enable both new life and old values, as well as new values and elements of our traditional lifestyle, I asked for silence in the halls, silence in the residence areas, silence in the chapel. And then we went on living with the noise, muted as it could be but there all the while — signs of new life coming in the doors.

The Vatican documents had become touchstones and guides to a new kind of an old life, another kind of human development, another way of being human and spiritual at the same time. Clearly, renewal was bringing with it a great deal more than an exercise in the internalization of new theological positions. What happened to women religious during the renewal period breached the borders of theory. This new territory guaranteed life for the living. How many religious were still alive enough of soul to risk it became another question. For those for whom renewal became a solemn obligation, rather than a risk, however, there were no limits to what could now be done in the name of God.

Feminism

The whole church had been called to renewal, of course. But for women religious the period touched every part of their lives in special ways — their prayer life, their community life, their social life, and their professional life were all stretched beyond the old limits.

Most of all, perhaps, renewal touched their notion of themselves as people, as adults, as women. These areas, long ignored and largely repressed, became central to the argument about whether religious life demanded "sacrifice" or self-development. For centuries, sacrifice had been the standard of a good religious life, of good religious women. Now, with the impact of the human development movement on the church's own call to responsibility, new norms and ideals began to emerge.

Like women everywhere around them, they began to embrace a woman's sense of self. They saw themselves as *women* religious as well as *religious* women. The distinction was a crucial one that called on women to own the woman's agenda.

Women began to emerge from under the neutralizing effects of the anonymity that came with name changes and uniform clothing. Young girls who had been given "religious" names at the time of their clothing ceremonies — many of them masculine names, in fact, because male saints, who outnumber women saints two to one, had long been painted as stronger or more effective than women saints — returned, once permitted, to the use of their baptismal names.

Who they were before God, who they had been raised to be, came to matter more than the neuterizing personas they had assumed long after the baptismal commitment that had brought them to religious life in the first place.

But with the name came the person. With the renewed recognition of what it is to be a person, a woman, with a complex of feelings and free will and ideas and individual gifts, undermined the notion of nuns as interchangeable parts. Now women religious were no longer pawns in the hands of a system. Nor were they genderless. They were individuals — adult, free-standing, intelligent, educated, and competent women. They were adults responsible to God for the giving of their gifts. "I always knew I loved music," a sister said to me. "But I don't want to teach it. I only want to use it for liturgy." The difference was now clear: teaching was one gift; playing an instrument was often entirely another. Every woman who walked in the door of the monastery could not be assumed to be a teacher. Neither could she be assumed to be invisible, unthinking, or subordinate. Women were not children to be used in mechanical ways. The were not a labor force to be used for the sake of the system. They were intelligent, spiritual, and self-directing adults to be unleashed for the sake of the gospel.

Sisters began to appear in my office, grappling with the effects of sexual abuse when they were children; struggling with the institutional oppression that men heaped on women, on sisters, so casually; enraged by the public abuse wreaked on the women around them who were too powerless, too needy, too frightened at the thought of losing their jobs to protest the abuse they took in the corporate world, the commercial world, the public world. "I was abused by a man when I was four," a young sister told me, "and I've hated myself for it all my life. I did penance and I got a relic of Maria Goretti," she said, "but the feelings never go away." My head snapped up: "If you want help, don't come back in here till you get rid of the Maria Goretti relics," I said. "Maria Goretti is the church's message to women at the end of a war where one army after another raped its way across Europe. The message is that it would be better for a woman to be murdered than to be assaulted. That is a man's answer to rape, not a woman's! Pray to someone else." We were working this woman's thing out together now, all of us. And our answers were changing us in ways that were better for us — and better for the women around us too.

It was a time of learning, of coming to grips with who we were and who we could be. It was a dangerous and exciting time. There was no blueprint for it except the glory of creation and the will of God for each of us.

I got up every single morning knowing that we were holding together by sheer force of conviction, of commitment, of will. And I preferred that to being held together by fear or force. "Leave them alone and they'll come home," the child's verse had taught me, and I could see the truth of it daily. That does not mean that I didn't know that it could collapse at any time. "Do not overdrive the flock," the Rule said in one place. And in another, after spending twelve chapters prescribing the manner of prayer in great detail, "If anyone knows a better way, let them do it...." Leadership now was not about herding people into lines. It was about raising questions and then gathering them into problem-solving groups so they were enabled to answer them.

23

Giving Focus to Change

WHEN MY IDEAS about the self, the universe, and my own place in it shift, everything in life shifts with them. I become a new person. Then my sense of security, my definition of self, my core beliefs begin to take on different colors, different form. What I once needed to exist, I come to know, I don't need at all now. More, I simply walk out of that skin into another one. Even my ideas about God change and I find myself with a more cosmic God that is bigger than my past. My sense of what is and is not right, moral, necessary, possible for me moves me from one kind of life to another. My very soul expands to embrace a whole new universe in process.

That's exactly what happened to this world called "religious life" when the concepts on which it had been operating for almost a hundred years suddenly shifted in form and focus. The plinth upon which the tradition stood for centuries rocked and resettled in ways that could not possibly have been imagined only ten years before.

Ministry

The change in ministry that came with this shift in attitude about the value of the individual changed the image of the entire community. What's more, it changed it quickly. Parishes that had been accustomed to having eight nuns in an eight-room school, discovered that their package deal — you send so many nuns, we'll provide so many bedrooms — had ended.

In some cases, with the advent of open placement and the sister's obligation to choose and negotiate her own ministry rather than be assigned to the parish schools we'd been staffing since 1875, only one or two sisters reapplied for former teaching positions. Sometimes none at all.

Sometimes leaving an established parish position had something to do with strained relationships between sisters and pastors who, accustomed to thinking of themselves as the real school administrator, ran afoul of sister-educators. The ecclesiastical world discovered that sisters would no longer work in situations where their academic decisions were routinely overturned or their professional recommendations were regularly ignored. And sisters discovered that simply because they were nuns did not mean that bad temper, emotional pollution, and toxic personalities would be tolerated. Now ministry was about total commitment and personal conviction, about new preparation and reasons for being somewhere.

Sometimes leaving a teaching position had to do with burnout or age or, more likely, the inspired awareness that others could do what they had been doing but few could do the new things that clearly needed to be done in a society of the new poor. Sister Alice's commitment to changing Grandma Stewart's bandages every day and to caring for the rest of the African American community on Eleventh Street became a model for many of what one person could do. So they came into the office wanting to be artists, wanting to be spiritual directors, wanting to be canon lawyers, wanting to go to Africa to work in the missions, wanting to do work in the bush in Alaska, wanting to start Benedictines for Peace in every monastery across the country.

In each case, I took a deep breath. To say yes was to take one more step into dispersion of our resources, one more step away from what had always been a clearly discernible center, one more step into what looked like individualism in a group that claimed community. But at the same time, these were, after all, small shards of the answer to the question about finding the things we "grew up for." There was only one possible answer: "Of course, try it," I'd say. "Then, we'll look at it in a year and see what it's telling us." Why? Because inside me burned an intuition for a chaos theory that the scientists hadn't named yet. I believed that what people really wanted to do, by and large, they could do. And they always did. "Sisters aren't doing what sisters should do," the critics said. "They're simply doing their own thing." And I said, "No, sisters are not doing 'their own thing.' Sisters are now doing what God gave them the abilities to do best."

Ironically enough, the identification of individual gifts did not limit or diminish the notion of service. If anything, it increased it. The expansion of ministries that came as individuals struck out with new energy into new areas of service changed the character of the community itself overnight. Artists, nurses, educational specialists, lecturers, activists, administrators, spiritual directors, musicians, counselors, catechists, social service personnel emerged out of what had been a heretofore basically uniform body of elementary and secondary school teachers.

I admit that there were moments when I knew without doubt that Mother Sylvester's administration of routine had to be easier than trying to steer a "community of individuals." Like any other oxymoron — bittersweet, deafening silence, square circle — the concept contained within itself two apparent contradictories. I was convinced, however, that only a community of free people could be any kind of really effective community at all anymore. Until a woman was free to go, I was sure, she was not really free to stay. The trick was to free women to stay where they wanted to be but could not possibly abide if it did more to destroy them as people than it did to develop them.

In the process, women religious discovered that the spiritual life, the gospel, demanded more than just being hidden, invisible, passive, and nameless. Personal growth brought a new kind of public presence, a new kind of public responsibility. Once a labor force for the Catholic school system, they became animators of both public and private projects. They brought the spirit of the Vatican documents to groups both inside and outside the church. They became another kind of Catholic voice.

Ecumenism

Sister Mary Margaret Kraus had surprised both the city and the community in the late 1960s by opening the new monastery chapel to interfaith services and Lutheran celebrations. In the 1980s nuns began to join Protestant ministers, both men and women, in public advocacy programs for the poor, for peace, for civic progress. More than that, Protestant clergy began to join them as well. A Christian community, not just a Catholic community, gathered around the monastery and its programs. Ecumenism became a reality in ways no number of documents on the subject could ever provide. Now there was a witness to unity rather than a hope for unity at the Mount.

But cooperation, I felt strongly, was not enough. I had come from what was then euphemistically called "a mixed marriage" of an Irish-Catholic mother and a Presbyterian father. I knew that ceremonies did not really dissolve the distance churches themselves had built between one Christian community and the next. We needed more than that to carry this new ecumenical world to the country. We needed more than common prayer, more than respect for one another. We needed understanding. I began to engage speakers not simply from around the country but from other faith traditions as well to speak to us of the other voices of God on earth.

Speakers from other traditions came to the Mount to give lectures: Jim Wallis, Evangelical, on peace; Geshe la Sopa, Buddhist monk, on prayer; Thomas Hoyt, African American Methodist bishop, on racism; Arthur Waskow, Jewish rabbi, on biblical midrash and its relationship to Benedictine *lectio.*

For the Erie Benedictines, the whole world became a place inhabited by God and the community became a world in microcosm that witnessed to it.

With the development of the person and a new kind of immersion in the world, with the Vatican documents, not the catechism, as the new ground of theology, little by little the faith of the community matured. Religious life, we began to see, was a call to keep the great questions of the spirit and the dynamic of the gospel alive. It was not a bargain made in blood to secure a better life in a world to come. Where going into Protestant churches, let alone Buddhist temples or Muslim mosques, had ranked once among the major mortal sins of the faith, ecumenism and interfaith support became an imperative of the faith. Religious life and liturgy became a focal point of the concerns of the entire world.

Liturgy

If people came to the Mount for anything at all, I knew, it would be for prayer and Eucharist. If the sisters themselves were going to be able to sustain their own spiritual lives in a church in turmoil, in a society in which the development of women only highlighted even more their invisibility in what would soon be a priestless church, it could not be at the regular twenty-five-minute *pro forma* Eucharist. Spiritual development had to come first, not simply the regularity of the ritual.

We needed to get some control over our own spiritual lives. One chaplain after another had dictated our prayer schedule, our homiletic sustenance, our liturgical growth and theology. It was time to take responsibility for our own eucharistic theology and growth.

To do that I created two distinct liturgy committees, the first to be responsible for daily prayer so that the Office itself would become the center of the community life; the second to prepare the Sunday liturgies in the spirit of the liturgical year. The priest presider eventually became a team of diocesan men rather than one live-in chaplain in order to allow for a variety of celebration styles and homilies. The priest became the church official at the community Eucharist rather than the community's being an observer at the priest's Eucharist. Some priests were willing to be directed by a team of professional liturgists; some were not. But the community's spiritual life thrived.

The thirty-five sisters who lived and worked in the city drove seven miles every Sunday of the year, snow and all, to attend the community liturgy despite the fact that they lived within blocks of neighborhood parish churches. "Do you have to go to the Mount for Sunday Mass?" a sister from another community asked a Benedictine one day, a touch of horror in her voice. "If by that you mean, does Joan tell us that we have to be there, the answer is no. We don't go to the Mount for Eucharist because we have to go. We go because we *have* to go!"

The change of attitude brought with it a change in witness. The commitment now was to the life of Jesus, not to the organizational concerns of canon law. Law came to be seen as a guide, a beacon, a checkpoint, neither a straitjacket nor the ultimate measure of fidelity to the life.

Suddenly the doors of the Mount swung wide open to take the world in, as Benedictine communities centuries before had always done. People began to come regularly to the community for Eucharist, for spirituality programs, for private spiritual direction, for retreats, for centering prayer, for rest. No bills were sent. No restrictions were laid down. No references were vetted.

Families came to visit. The poor came to stay between housing projects. Parolees came for a kind of launching pad between jail and work. Children came for refuge. The sick and elderly began to come to the infirmary for emergency care. Infants were brought for foster care. Laypeople came for quiet and spiritual conversation. The Mount became a different place, more like the years of its founding, perhaps, when Benedicta Riepp, foundress, took in to live with the sisters the very children they were teaching.

And, just as important, the sisters went into the city. The first apartment experiment enlarged in scope to become a "hospitality house" for women in the old academy on Ninth Street. Eventually eight other small group living sites nested in the neighborhoods of the city, present to the people, present to the world, more aware of what it was to live in lower-middle-class America. Every small community was a praying, working, living echo of the larger monastery from which it sprang, just as were the parochial mission communities that had been opened by the community in the late 1800s to serve parishes miles away from Erie. The community became a leaven for many rather than a labor force for a few. We were a local community with a new national purpose, a new national profile, a new national awareness. We became committed to being an intense Christian community rather than a monastic museum. Behind it all, through it all, the Vatican documents took deep root.

The community gathered in chapel on any given night might easily be three to four spiritual or religious traditions gathered in prayer.

Scripture, the life of Jesus, became the litmus test of the valid life, not rules long arcane and no longer valuable.

Bishops, more peers now in the mission of the church than its lords and lawgivers, ceased to be the norm of community decisions or the measure of the community's charism. There were things that had to be done for which no Catholic institution existed. There were also Catholic institutions that could safely and securely be given into the care of laypeople so that sisters could go where families with small children and large debts could not afford to work. No amount of episcopal caution, no degree of control, could be allowed to obstruct their going.

The laity became partners in the work of the gospel. The very definition of "community" expanded to include, as the book of Acts did, "those who were of one mind and one heart," lay and religious alike. Laypeople began to teach the sisters as much as the sisters had ever taught them. "I remember," one sister said, "when two young theology teachers at the academy gave the first workshop on the Eucharist for the community. It was shocking — and challenging — to have someone else interpret the Eucharist for us in such a different way. I began to see that global consciousness is required by the Eucharist itself. It changed me." Clearly the "role of the laity" had begun to take root.

The Erie Benedictines became a community of heart large enough, close enough, unified enough to extend themselves beyond any artificial barriers. The Mount sent sisters out to the world true to the prayers they prayed that God would send help to the poor — to Ethiopia, to Mexico, to Alaska, to El Salvador, to Nicaragua, to Colombia. Sisters went year after year, place after place. In the end, they shrank our world and they stretched us too. The Catholic ghetto disappeared and in its place had come a world full of the grandeur of God.

24

Fragmentation

THE OTHER SIDE OF CHANGE

I N RETROSPECT the process of renewal comes out looking clean and clear. In reality, the process was dense and disorderly. Historical time-lines do not tell the story. False starts or concerted impediments marked everything.

Plans were barely made, resolutions were hardly written, until they didn't apply anymore. Or couldn't be applied. Or were simply ignored in deference to the immediate or the enticing. Those who "couldn't wait around much longer" quietly began to live outside the borders of the resolutions. Those who feared that the community would simply cease to exist without the mainstays of the familiar worked every idea to the bone in hopes of finding the last wall beyond which renewal dare not go.

Like any institution in the throes of death and the gasping for life, every new move had a touch of spasm to it, every response a knee-jerk reaction. Little that happened, happened easily or smoothly or without some kind of point and counterpoint. Whatever happened, one way or the other, out of one theology or the next, one Vatican council or the other, either the bishop complained or the people complained or the pastors complained or some part of the community complained.

When the sisters themselves began to plan the liturgies for the Mount, for instance — in accordance with the latest approved liturgical documents of the time — the bishop called me to a meeting to forbid such things, only to discover we had not broken a single liturgical law. We did, we told him as we showed him the Vatican documents that suggested such adaptations, often change the way of proclaiming the readings through song or drama or dance or dialogue interpretations in order to bring fresh meaning to the text. Some laypeople asked at the end of Mass whether they had been at Mass or not, and vowed never to come back to the Mount chapel — so they could be sure of their orthodoxy. But others, relieved to find life where only rote had been for years, not only came back; they brought the rest of their family with them. Finally, four carloads of sisters left the Mount every Sunday to attend Mass in a neighboring parish where only the priest was actively involved in either the Liturgy of the Word or the Liturgy of the Eucharist.

Every week the community liturgist talked to individuals about their concerns. Every week I sat in the office and wrestled in my heart over the distress. How do you renew a liturgy if you're never permitted to change it? And how do you help people who are suffering because you do change it?

In the end, individual differences threatened the life of the community even more than theological renewal did. Some people "knew" what needed to be done. Some people questioned why anything else had to be done at all. I thought for awhile that there was no way through the morass. For some, questions were not acceptable; for others, answers were not admissible.

Fragmentation became the order of the day. Over the years, the community had drifted into self-reinforcing groups defined by ideology. Where work groups had once crossed age levels and living groups had always crossed educational backgrounds and social groups crossed social origins, now sisters organized themselves theologically between those who wanted certain changes and those who did not.

Group communication was civil at best. Confused by the amount of resistance in each camp, people clung to the people who understood them, who agreed with them, who wanted what they wanted. Renewal had made strange bedfellows of us all.

The Catholic community itself became part of the larger audience and various support systems, cheering on one side or the other, planting their own flags on various topics. Some wanted sisters in a habit; others did not. Some wanted sisters only in the schools; others felt the need for religious to broaden their base of involvements, to speak out, to become part of the larger society.

The pressures of partisan support from outside the monastery affected the community in some cases as did the theory. As changes within religious life became more and more public, Catholic friends and family made it clear what was and was not acceptable to them. The need to confront attitudes about religious life that were as firmly entrenched outside the community as well as within it became paramount. Society itself, after all, was in the middle of a sea change of ideals. Flower children had rejected the values of the social system as the Western world had known them for almost fifty years. Police in riot gear were hosing down the best and the brightest of U.S. university students. The world was poised on the brink of another war, this one more than likely terminal.

Lay Catholics who had been defending the faith to a hostile Protestant world for generations had no desire in the midst of civil unrest to deal with changes in the church too. Change, after all, was for some tantamount to admitting that Protestants had been right all along about things as essential to the Catholic tradition as the Eucharist, abstinence from meat on Fridays, weekly confession, or Latin as the only possible language of consecration. And now, it seemed, they were right about religious life as well.

The theological confusion that resulted from Vatican II affected religious as much as it affected the serious layperson. If religious life, its purpose and its eternal value, could be upended so easily, so totally, so quickly, did the life have any value at all any more? If it wasn't, after all, a "higher" vocation, if it didn't carry special privilege, if it wasn't the Olympian dimension of the Christian life, then what was left of it? In fact, had it ever had real value at all?

What's worse, the loss of theological support from the larger community translated into a loss of support for the ministries of the community. As sisters became more and more involved in civil issues — poverty, women's issues, legislative issues — that jeopardized the lives of hundreds of thousands of people everywhere, they found that they had inherited other sets of opponents as well.

What religious were meant to do as well as what they were meant to be or how they were meant to live and dress and work became major problems. The community found itself uncertain not just about the involvement of sisters in public programs but about the very situations themselves.

What were "some of our sisters" doing carrying placards at peace rallies? This was America, after all, the messianic center of the universe. We couldn't possibly be wrong in our foreign policy, in our treatment of other peoples, in our motives. And anyway, what were sisters doing in "politics"?

What did the individual members of the community themselves think about racism. "I'm from Virginia," Sister Francis Claire said. "I can't help what I think. I was brought up that way." Point made: born Christian but brought up southern white where slavery had been read for centuries as a biblical truth. Baptism, it became clear, was no substitute for conversion and the Bible no simple answer to the questions of the time.

The social confusion became as much a factor in the renewal of religious life as the theological confusion of the time. The whole world was a work in progress. Ideas about the universe, the limits of science, the role of secularism in the religious state, the need for some kind of universal law, and the integration of peoples everywhere became more and more urgent in their demands.

Norms and values could no longer be taken for granted, not even in defined groups like ours. Demands for change and hopes for adjustment jousted everywhere. All the old answers were being tested, tried, judged — one at a time. Conformity and compliance wrestled for dominance in every institution. "Go along," maybe; change, no. Nothing claimed to be like it used to be and the social ruptures the changes caused played on every TV set in the country — in the world — every night.

Every social institution swerved and thrashed about aimlessly at the same time. Government, education, marriage and family life, religion, economics, science, and social structure all tossed and heaved on a sea of discontinuities. Institutions tried in vain to legislate some way to maintain the status quo for themselves — and all of them lost the contest. Students contested with teachers, children divorced their parents, laypeople formed their own faith-sharing groups, priests left to marry, nuns left to be treated like adults. The tectonic plates of the planet on which the world had rested firm for so long now creaked and began to move.

Governments, both democratic and totalitarian, fell everywhere. Educational theory shifted from authoritarian to permissive. Role distinctions in marriage and society came under attack and began to crumble under the assault as a newly redefined woman's movement picked up steam. Science began to talk about creating and recreating life rather than simply saving it or charting it or exploring it. Economics discovered that when the poor get poorer the security of the rich begins to erode. Religions came face to face with other religions and the absolutist claims of each. Social structures groaned and heaved under the stress of adjustments. And while whole strains of the world began to seep through old borders, whole new military systems arose to maintain the status quo.

So what was the purpose of religious life anyway? And even more than that, in a sense, what was the purpose of community life now? Sisters could do anything they wanted to do, so why live with a group of strangers to do it?

At one point in time, women's lives were defined out of the public arena, with the exception of nursing and teaching —

and even those interests, for the most part, were simply temporary adjuncts to marriage and motherhood. To be a sister then was to be a special kind of woman, someone who stepped into a kind of time warp of the holy and the blessed. Now the time warp was rapidly disappearing. The obvious and the common had reasserted itself, blurred all distinctions, leveled the spiritual enterprise.

Laywomen could do anything a nun could do now: read the scriptures at Mass, be Eucharistic ministers, teach in the Catholic school. On top of all that, she could do it in her own apartment, on her own money, and with her own car. So why this? Why community? Why live with strangers to do what you could easily do on your own?

The questions plagued women to the center of their souls. Now the questions were not about the way we did things. They were about whether or not it was worthwhile trying to do anything at all.

25

Revitalization

THE CAPSTONE OF RENEWAL

THERE ARE THOSE who say that institutional renewal is, at best, a contradiction in terms. By the time groups become aware of the need to change rather than simply to make adjustments, these theorists argue, the institution already lacks the energy — the vision — it takes to effect real change. Then like buggy whip makers in a Model-T world, they simply die out. One at a time. Slowly. Sometimes for a period of years. Renewal means refounding, in other words, not refurbishing.

Worse than the lack of resources in a group, however, is the kind of institutional neuroses that can paralyze once-successful organizations. The concept of institutional neurosis has been only relatively recently applied to organizations and may, in fact, be no more scientifically certifiable organizationally than it is with persons. But, like beauty, it's something we know when we see it.

Neurotic organizations, like neurotic individuals, according to researchers, take their norms from outside themselves rather than from within the group itself. They rely on past visions of the organization, outside authorities, platitudes and prescriptions, rather than on their own vision for the future. They simply go on, doing what they've always done, whether it is working or not, whether it has any present meaning or not. And those who stay in these organizations do it without questioning.[13]

For years, until Vatican II, in fact, women religious inherited a system that was vacuum packed, preserved from eras before them, a fossil of ages past.

When it's clear that the system is no longer producing at the level to which they are accustomed rather than reassess their situation and focus their resources on what they can do to change the situation, neurotic organizations, like neurotic individuals, blame someone else for their predicament. The church won't allow them to change, they say. The culture won't accept it. Or, they argue, people expect something different from them. So the product never improves, the structures never get updated, the organization never changes. And it's not, they're sure, their own lack of vision, education, courage, or willingness that is at fault. It's just the way things are.

Content to continue with the system as it was rather than raise questions, insist on review, or create new systems themselves, religious communities watched woman after woman leave religious life and insisted on blaming the "secularism" of the society, or the "loss of faith" in this generation, or the lack of family support of vocations. Seldom did religious suggest that they themselves, the form of life as they were living it, might be the problem.

Neurotic organizations, however, can also function in a manner just the opposite of rigid withdrawal. They can just as easily, in their eagerness to update, lose their identity entirely by becoming just like everybody else. They have no special character, nothing whatsoever to give to the world that people can't get anywhere else.

There is nothing about them that makes them necessary. They can be quaint, they can be rare, but they are not really significant to the world around them. Or they can make just what everybody else makes, do just what everybody else does, offer nothing of unique value to the world. Just more of the same.

In 1922, when the church homogenized religious life, imposed the same schedules, ministries, prayer forms, even clothing styles, on all of them, women religious simply accepted the single form of "active" orders or "cloistered" orders

as more authentic than the very particular reasons for which
they had been founded and approved by the church itself in
centuries past. The various charisms or models of the Christ
life — Benedictine community, Franciscan poverty, Domini-
can preaching, apostolic service — became blurred into one
large organization wearing different colors of clothes or shape
of headgear.

Neurotic organizations often know that they have become
useless or retrograde or stuck. But instead of doing something
about it, they simply spend their days blaming themselves. "We
know we should do something else," they cry, as if crying were
enough to make them worthy of salvage, "but we really don't
know what it is." They do no dreaming, they allow no group
reflection, they encourage no new ideas. In fact new ideas, new
ways of doing things, new ways of living frighten them. They
simply sit and watch life pass them by.

"We're dying out now," a sister told me in 1968. "Religious
life will disappear soon. The best we can do is simply to live
it out." And the communities have indeed gotten smaller and
smaller as the years have gone by, no new works attempted, no
new kind of public presence or new interests developed or new
community commitment. They have been faithful to prayer,
generous in service but they don't have a clue why the few
women who have come over the years have also left by now.

Finally, some neurotic organizations, like neurotic people,
live inside a fantasy. "This will all pass," they promise. "This
is a fad," they're sure. "The present situation is really not as
bad as people say."

Then the members sit on the fence waiting to see which side
wins, the past or the present. They take no risks. They make a
few cosmetic changes. But they build nothing new. They begin
no new initiatives. The grumbling gets worse by the year. The
joy goes out of living. The energy wanes. Institutional depression sets in with a vengeance. People coast and go through the
motions and cut corners. They find a nice comfortable niche in
which to hide — a plum position, an easy job, a routine task —
and they resign themselves to living it out. "I'll stay," they say,

"as long as I have a job or as long as it's something to do or as long as I can."

They withdraw inward. They pull down the curtains of their souls. They wait for the storm to be over. It's not an uncommon posture in any organization that doesn't know what to do next or how to do it. What was once one of the major music stores in town put up a window display ten years ago and has never changed it since. Nor have they changed anything else in the store, none of the instruments, none of the music. The store is dark now, even when the sign says open.

In the neurotic organization, glorification of the past becomes an occupation in itself. The celebration of yesterday takes hold of a group like a vise. In religious circles, more energy goes into caring for the heritage room than into the tasks of the time. Instead, their old ministries decline, get smaller, become shadows of their former selves. No activities or projects or buildings are closed and renovated and opened under new impulse. They simply die, treading water, suspended in midair, looking after an era that has long since passed.

They fantasize about a future that will never come. They promise it to themselves. They refuse to believe that it won't. And all the while they ignore the problems of the present.

Religious communities have gone through all of this and more during the period of renewal. Shocked by the rapidity of change, the lack of clear direction, they have been tempted to stop halfway to the goal. Groups made ornamental changes — new jobs here, new clothes there, yes — but the old image of religious life hung like a ghost over their heads. They changed their habits but not their hearts, their language but not their ideas. Secretly they yearned for a past that would never return, a theology that could never return in the same style, to the same degree, it had existed in the past.

Some groups, out of a kind of holy nostalgia, even tried to reclaim old customs. But all to little or no avail beyond the comfort that holding on to the familiar might bring a group whose "good old days" are all in the past.

In Erie, the situation in 1978 was ripe for just such maneuvers. The years of renewal had taken their toll, both in energy and in relationships. After years of study in organizational theory and change, I could see the ennui setting in; I could feel it in the halls, I could hear it in the conversations. People were happy that the worst was over, but what had happened as a result of all the so-called "renewal"?

I was sitting in a group discussion on the future needs of the community. The question had been designed as part of the discernment process for the election of 1978, the election at which I would eventually become the next prioress. We had done well together in the discussion on the present achievements of the community. We knew we had weathered the hard core polarization that the renewal process had brought with it. We knew we had healed the divisions, rebuilt the friendships, recast the group. But the future, it seemed, faced us gray and blank. "Why are we here?" a younger sister said with a kind of despair in her voice. "What's the use of it? What are we doing that anybody else can't do, too?"

The question crystallized the problem of the future in one short sentence. Why be a sister, a community, anymore? We didn't have the answer in that group, but I knew without doubt that it was the determining question of the time. I began what would become a three-year study of the relationship between religious ministry and the social system of the times.[14] That study became the foundation for an article called "Ministry and Secularism" on the notion of a corporate commitment.

The process of revitalization, I knew, at least in large stable groups, depends on two things: commitment to the vision of a new future and, at the same time, a genuine respect for the past. Revitalization is not a cultural revolution. It does not set out, like Mao Tse-Tung's young revolutionaries, to destroy everything that went before it.

Revitalization, on the contrary, sets out to channel old energy, now dissipated, into new directions. Without that, the entire enterprise, no matter how satisfied a group might be with itself, no matter how stable it may look, cannot possibly survive the kind of sweeping ecclesiastical and cultural changes that were pushing and pulling religious life after Vatican II. One purpose gone, another purpose had to be not only defined but compelling.

Erie had the internal and spiritual attributes, if they so chose, to make the transition. The community had never strayed far from the basics. When it seemed that everything in the life had been changed, the fact remained that it had not. Whatever the pressures or ideological divisions in the group, there had never been a call either to abandon community life (still practiced in both large and small groups) or to forego choral prayer (still scheduled for at least almost two hours a day) as the two basics of Benedictine life. The age-old position of prioress, too, remained unchallenged. The recommendation to turn the title "prioress" into "administrator" for the sake of social relevance and lay understanding passed the chapter but never really became common coin. "Administrators," we knew, had something to do with corporations; prioresses had something to do with communities. The tradition remained intact; only the historical accidentals had really been changed.

Transition demands both discontinuity and continuity at the same time. My own early experiences had given me an overview of religious life that began with the heady giddiness of Vatican II, with all its potential, all its excitement. Then, it left me immersed in the hard work of translating the theology of renewal into the politics of renewal at the local level everywhere. My experiences of religious life from the age of thirty-five on were not simply local. They gave me a point of view regarding the entire plain of church and religious life everywhere. These were the years, I joked, "when the federation was teaching me how to be a prioress."

The problem was that everywhere around me I saw frustration, anger, neurosis, and goodwill going to dust. One community after another grappled with the prospect of division. Just when we all needed high energy and committed resources most, groups exhausted by the fray were splitting off from one another in the hope that when internal peace came new energy would come with it.

Benedictine prioresses especially, who normally lived in closer contact with their communities than the presidents and provincials of larger, more widespread congregations, were showing the wear and tear of the daily pressures of the process. The great ideas spawned at the level of theoretical discussions in Chapter committees dissolved once they got back home. In their offices, when they were alone, where there was little of the same kind of vision or support or understanding of the urgency of the situation, it became enough simply to get through the day without the kinds of crises that came in a polarized community. Surely, I thought, there had to be another way.

At the same time, I had a younger community to work with and the continuing support of Mary Margaret's presence and encouragement in the new administration. I appointed her as consultant to the council in the early years of the administration and then as director of the community conference center. As a result, what the community saw was continuity in action, not a rupture of direction. I was simply walking a path that had already been laid, not striking out on my own. I was simply doing what I could to complete what had already been well begun.

I was following a woman who had taken the buffeting daily and went on loving all of us regardless. Any lesser person would have loved none of us by the time it was over. But adolescence is an aggravating time in any family and we were in it, trying to learn to be mature religious, trying to learn to be new kinds of ministers, trying to learn to be adult women. I was committed to continuing the process even on the days when the cost of doing so seemed far greater than the worth of it. Things were happening. People were growing. New life was possible. But the stress of change was a long way from over. It was going to take a lot more trust to get us through it. Though I was not as soft, not as yielding, not as nonthreatening as Mary Margaret had been, I had a good sense of humor, a great love of life, a good understanding of the situation, and a deep trust in the self-correcting quality of a group. I like fun and parties and a good laugh and I sought them out, no matter who had been sour with me that day. She would feel better tomorrow, I thought — and hopefully, so would I.

Like Mary Margaret, too, I didn't have to have all the answers. I had simply to allow the questions. Surely if I tried hard enough, I could enable the community to continue its journey to new life. My model was not conquest and control. "The flock should not be overdriven," I read over and over again in the Rule. My model in Mary Margaret and in that Rule became genuine respect for the wisdom of the group and openness to the challenge of the times. We could do this together and we could be a monastery in the style of the great ones of earlier ages that lived the life and gave life to the world around them at the same time.

But for an enterprise of such crucial proportions, I had only two possible strategies in mind: a participative process that would engage and capture the wisdom of the entire group and a deep-seated commitment to personal creativity. The community had to be involved in everything so that they could own it, and I had to allow creativity to run wild. My own gift had to be reckless trust in the vision of the group and the creativity of its individual members. Then maybe some small seed would "fall on good ground" and grow again.

Members, I knew, hold more power in an organization than they realize. No leader can revitalize an institution that does not want to be revitalized. Divided organizations, resistant organizations, passive-aggressive organizations die even when they have the ability to live. The community in Erie had been all of those things once. But we had come beyond that now.

Transformation and revitalization begins in the heart of the membership, and these hearts were open. The membership, not the leader alone, is the real and final answer to revitalization. One of the functions of genuine leadership in contrast to administrative control is simply to enable it to happen. Lao-Tzu, Chinese Taoist philosopher, once wrote: "When leaders are good, then the people say, 'We did it ourselves.' "

The equation is clear: if the future of a group depends on the ideas of one person, when that one person runs out of ideas, and that person will, the future of the group grinds to a slow but certain halt.

Only one thing I knew for sure: I knew we had to do more with less. We were getting older, getting smaller, getting poorer by the day. Most of all, I knew we had to do it together. We ourselves, as a community, had to become the sign of a religious life that no longer depended on the aesthetics of symbol for either social power or public privilege.

26

A Time of Beginning Again

EVERY FIVE YEARS the community is required to make a report to the federation on the current character and concerns of the community. In 1983, the report was entitled "Seasons of Growth." Things began to happen in 1978 that forever broke the century-old image of the semicloistered teaching Benedictines in lower eastside Erie. Public participation came as new territory for us. In 1950, when I enrolled in high school at St. Benedict Academy, I, and most of the city, had never heard of the Erie Benedictines. After 1978, everybody in the city had heard about the Erie Benedictines, and what they heard was often not to their liking.

To me this immersion in the public arena seemed both imperative and inevitable. If we were going to be a religious community, there was no other direction to take. It was the very direction, in fact, out of which the nice, settled, comfortable religious life we'd all known before Vatican II had originally come. It simply took a long time for any of us to realize how involved Benedictinism had always been in public life. I myself never realized how deeply rooted responsibility for the public pursuit of justice was in my own psyche until the General Chapter of 1978. It was my last chapter as federation president and a very painful one.

In the first place, I was leaving the position of president to become prioress in Erie, a change I had neither considered nor wanted.

In the second place, the chapter itself was in turmoil. "Getting the Justice Issues in Focus," the theme for the Chapter meeting, had been developed and accepted by the group a year before this, at the regular pre-Chapter preparatory meeting. At the Chapter itself, however, when the discussion and recommendations that emerged began to suggest that communities become publicly engaged in peace and justice issues, the threat level soared.

This was a group for which schools had been their only work for almost a century. Their sisters were trained for education. Their monies had all been invested in school buildings. Their properties were tied up in residence halls and facilities. Justice issues and education, as far as they were concerned, were light years apart.

"Whose agenda is this?" a prioress demanded to know. "Ours or Joan Chittister's and the LCWR's?" It was a stunning blow, one for which I was totally unprepared. Yes, the LCWR had for years struggled with the role of religious in a world wracked with injustice. And yes, I had indeed been talking for years about the need for religious to consider new ministries, but I had done nothing to impose that on anyone — in fact, no one was more surprised, or more delighted — when that topic emerged in the pre-Chapter. Nor had I had anything to do with the final structure of the Chapter agenda. In fact, it was the prioress from Kentucky who had suggested both the theme and the title. So why would it be attributed to me, and why would I be so disconcerted by the fact that it had been?

Later that evening, trying to relieve the strain of the meeting over nachos at a local Mexican restaurant, the group in idle conversation discovered the fact that one of the house customs of the Erie community was to give a "title" to newly professed sisters. It's purpose, we explained, was to emphasize a personal strength or encourage its development. I had been totally uninspired by mine.

Of the seven newly professed sisters that year, I was the only one whose title had nothing to do with the then current understandings of St. Benedict: others in the group got titles like "the

Humility of St. Benedict," "the Prayerfulness of St. Benedict," "the Obedience of St. Benedict," "the Listening of St. Benedict." I could hardly wait to see what my own would be. As the youngest in the group, I received mine last. I could feel my face fall the minute I opened the envelope. Mine, as far as I could see at the age of twenty-one, had nothing to do with St. Benedict. But I did know that I didn't dare let the prioress see the disappointment in me. I put the envelope away and never thought of it again.

"Well," the group wanted to know, "what was it!" "My title," I said offhandedly, "is Sister Joan Chittister, . . ." I paused, thunderstruck as I realized what I was about to say. "My title," I went on, more slowly and more thoughtfully now, "is Sister Joan Chittister of the Justice of St. Benedict."

What was happening in Erie, what was happening in this General Chapter, made perfect sense to me, maybe had always made perfect sense to me. The commitment to justice was of the essence, was the direction I'd been given, even when I didn't realize it. In fact, I could not read the gospels and think of any other way to go if religious life was going to be relevant, if religious life was going to be true. And more, if Benedictine life was going to be Benedictine. What else had Benedictinism been about over the centuries if not justice for the poor, justice for the sick, justice for the peasants, justice for the illiterate? What else then were we ourselves to be about?

The changes in public presence, in ministry — the new directions taken by religious across the country, in fact — became conscious changes. They were deliberate. They were calculated. If you were going by the standards common to religious life before Vatican II, they were also dangerous. The public didn't like many of them. The clergy didn't like most of them. Even some community members still shuddered at the thought of some of the things that were happening. Sisters were becoming involved in antiwar demonstrations. Some went to jail. Sisters began to march with the black community for civil rights. Sisters took part in public prayer services, in public peace vigils, in public petitions, in public teach-ins on social issues. For those for whom the change in clothing seemed ill-conceived, the changes in ministry were nothing short of scandalous. All of it was done in the pursuit of justice — but to pursue "justice" in the United States was to question the very forces of the establishment that were its unassailables: industrial interests, government lobbies, and the military budget and policies. Dwight Eisenhower had warned the American public on his way out of office that "the military-industrial complex" constituted the gravest problem in the United States. Few people understood then what he was talking about; even fewer people listened. But every day more and more people, including Americans, began to be affected: lives changed; social services changed; American foreign policy changed. Who was going to challenge such a worldview if not the religious of the world and Benedictines, of all people?

Benedictines are stable and autonomous groups of religious who, for the most part, live in the same monastery in the same part of the world their entire lives. Whatever happens to the people and the place around them happens to them too. When the industries leave that place, or the lake sours there, or the land turns to dust — when the economy shrinks or shrivels — their operations shrink and shrivel as well. The fate of the area determines the fate of the monastery. The fortunes of a Benedictine monastery rise and fall with the fortunes of the area it serves.

It cannot be true, then, that simply because of the basic contemplative nature of the Benedictine lifestyle that Benedictines can be aerily disinterested in the world around them. On the contrary. Justice must be the hallmark, the conscience, of the Benedictine whose whole life is rooted in the scriptures — the psalms, the prophets, the life of Jesus. Otherwise, the learnings of that life cannot possibly be either spiritual or real.

Our role as Benedictines, we were beginning to understand, was to be exactly what we had been from the beginning — a voice for the poor and oppressed. With the gospel as the filter for every action we took, whole new directions became clear. Dangerous, but clear.

The Erie Benedictines had embarked on a whole new way of being community, a whole new way of bringing a Benedictine presence to the area and the world in which they lived.

Like the process of becoming conscious of "the needs of the members," the changes in ministry weren't easy either. Long-time benefactors, disturbed at the challenge to American politics implied by the positions taken by the community against nuclearism, in behalf of the poor, for the sake of the equality of women, withdrew their support. Catholics who had said little or nothing about the internal changes taking place in religious communities criticized the public dimensions roundly. Local clergy who had been dismayed about the apparent loss of religious life signaled by the loss of religious symbols were doubly dismayed by the emergence of women religious in the affairs of the time. Some even wrote letters to the editor themselves in criticism of our positions.

Nevertheless, the attention of the community now focused on making a conscious commitment to respond to "the signs of the times" out of continuing respect for a past that had made Benedictinism central to the world around it.

Popes had for centuries credited the Benedictine order for having saved civilization during the Dark Ages. With the breakdown of the Roman empire and the collapse of its borders, foreigners poured into the empire, conquered its outposts, and corrupted its institutions. As time went by, Benedictine abbeys became the only stable institutions left in Europe. Whole towns grew up around them that stand to this day as monuments to the role of Benedictinism in society. The monks preserved the manuscripts, taught peasants how to farm, opened hostels for the sick and for travelers, collected alms from toll roads to provide the West's first welfare programs, adjudicated social conflicts, and organized schools. The schools remained over the centuries, in a period when literacy was at a premium and education was for the upper classes only, a hallmark of the order.

But now, here, in this century, schools — at least the classic K-12 configuration of them — were now mainstream, now compulsory. No child was excluded from the public system now. For Benedictines not to respond again to new and more threatening attacks on education, on the culture itself, was perhaps far more irreligious than it was for them to become involved in the signs of the times around us, however comfortable it had become to escape behind private school walls. John XXIII had identified the "signs of the times" as global poverty, nuclear disarmament, and the emergence of women. But what did those mean to us sitting in small town USA on previously walled property with little history of public involvement beyond elementary and secondary education? Three months after the election, I set about finding out.

Every sister in the community responded to a questionnaire that asked her to name what she saw as the major issue facing the world and how she thought it did or did not relate to Benedictinism, to us. The topics coalesced around five issues: housing, women's issues, hunger, peace, and ecology.

Each of them had a special relationship to Benedictine history or charism. Housing recalled the Benedictine tradition of hospitality to pilgrims. Hunger reminded us of the contribution of the order to the maintenance of European agriculture. The ecology question echoed for us the long involvement of Benedictine abbeys in the reclamation of land in Europe. Women's issues brought with them a new appreciation of the fact that Benedictinism was the first joint religious order of men and women in the history of the church. Peace, the oldest and most universal Benedictine motto, came from the order that not only stressed interior peace in its devotion to the spiritual life but had actually provided houses of refuge for the poor and were makers of what came to be known as the first attempt to control war.

In August 1978 the community went through five different workshops conducted by members of the community who were already personally involved in one of these five key issues of the late twentieth century. At the end of the workshop weekend, the community voted on two proposals. The first proposal dealt simply with whether, as a group, we wanted to concentrate on some kind of public service together or would we each simply go on doing good things but doing them independently. The second proposal depended on the first. If we chose to work on some issue together, what would it be?

The answer to the first proposal was unanimous: there was no purpose staying in the group if it did not enable us to do something together that we could not do alone. Yes, we wanted to be about something significant together.

The answer to the second question became far more difficult. We were not trying to choose between good and evil. That would be easy. We were trying to choose between good and good. That was impossible.

In the end, we simply decided that we would "cast lots" and whatever issue received the highest number of votes we would all support. The community vote split all five ways. There were 29 votes cast in favor of housing as our corporate commitment, 28 for hunger, 27 for women, 30 for poverty. Peace received 31 votes of the 145 votes cast.

At that moment, the Benedictine Sisters of Erie, longtime teachers in the Diocese of Erie, in the style of the great Benedictines centuries before them, transformed themselves into a peace community with a corporate commitment to nuclear disarmament. With that simple decision — on the strength of one vote — everything became difficult but everything became clear as well.

We knew what we were about again. And it touched everything we did from the simple to the sublime.

Public prayer changed to include a consciousness of nuclear policies and nuclear threat.

The council and I, in a community with barely enough money to pay its own bills, began to tithe to support groups whose sole purpose was nuclear disarmament and conflict resolution strategies.

We changed the community stationery to include the tagline, "Give Peace a Chance."

Sisters from every facet of the community began to participate in public peace demonstrations as representatives of the community itself. Some of them even did civil disobedience.

Every sister in the community, whatever ministry she did privately, took as her personal responsibility the need to use that work somehow to promote world peace and to argue for the denuclearization of the country.

Every year at a "Blessing of Ministries" ceremony we each pledged both to do our own private ministry and to support the corporate commitment by some specific action. I wrote, for instance, "I, Joan Chittister, will spend my gifts and talents this year as prioress of the community and I will support the corporate commitment by doing public speaking and writing on this subject throughout the year."

Each of us did something specific that bound all of us together in one great common commitment to bring the will of God for peace in the world in one specific way. The principal of the community academy refused to allow military recruiters on campus. First grade teachers began twin Peace Crane projects with elementary schools in Japan. Sister Mary Alice, who could not do civil disobedience, did dishes for those who did. Sister Irene held bake sales of her famous bread to help pay for the busses that took sisters to national demonstrations.

The community printed "Our Lady, Queen of Peace" holy cards to insert in community mail. The back of them carried a quotation from John XXIII: "Nuclear weapons are a sin against humanity."

Sisters even went to Washington to lobby the National Conference of Catholic Bishops in an all-night prayer vigil to support the proposed American Bishops' Peace Pastoral, "The Challenge of Peace: God's Promise and Our Response," which many of the bishops, past military men themselves, strongly opposed.

We put up "Nuclear Free Zone" signs on all our buildings both at the monastery and in the neighborhoods in town in which the sisters lived.

We walked eight miles through the city every Good Friday, saying public stations in front of the armory, the federal building, the topless bar, the soup kitchen, the General Electric plant — all places that symbolized the culture of violence that left people both around the world and in our own neighborhoods frightened for their futures, impoverished in the present, and invisible in the public arena.

Sisters demonstrated at the Pentagon, marched in peace rallies in New York City, held die-ins on the steps of the local cathedral to bring attention to the possibility of the nuclear holocausts we were planning in order, we said, to "defend" ourselves.

I even asked the community how they would feel about it if I myself engaged in civil disobedience and wound up in jail. Then, having their support, I fell and broke my ankle, not once but twice, and never did get to jail. Going to jail may well have been some sisters' gift to the world; it clearly was not meant to be mine.

And I took the phone calls that criticized us for doing all those things. "You have a lunatic fringe in that community," one businessman told me. "As a Catholic, it's embarrassing to me to see them on the streets. You better get a hold of that," he finished with an edge to his voice. I thought a minute. "I want to thank you for your support," I said. "We've never been accused of being Christian before."

But the criticism began to take a new shape too. A company that had hung the banners advertising the summer festival on which we depended to pay our food bills between academic years refused to do it anymore. Parents removed their children from our high school. Old friends ceased to come to the Mount anymore. Talk show hosts made fun of us daily on a local radio program.

Justice became our passion, our habit, our sign, our bond. Through it all, the future became clearer as we went. There was so much to do — and we did it together.

The list was a long one: We became the national headquarters of Pax Christi, USA, the international Catholic peace movement. We changed the liturgy to include a role for women. We opened the monastery to ministries for the poor. We turned the children's camp into a year-round conference center so that people in the area could have access to one of the only public pieces of land on the lake. We became part of the Sanctuary movement in order to deal with political refugees from Central America whom the Reagan administration had declared illegal aliens. We began to expand the new monastery we had just built in order to be able to take in guests for retreats and rest. We absorbed a small Benedictine community of twenty-one sisters from Wisconsin whose lives were full of energy but who lacked the money or the ministry to go on supporting themselves. We drilled a natural gas well at a time of oil shortages to test the degree of gas available in the area.

Over the next twelve years, the corporate commitment was reviewed and nuanced three times to include issues of poverty, ecology, and the oppression of women that are direct by-products of a society that espouses violence as its road to peace.

The pressures on us for doing these things approached the unbearable. In the early years, we were almost entirely alone in our positions in the area. We were called communists, traitors, femi-nazis, crazies. But the sisters went on. Regardless. And together.

Did I impose the justice issue on the federation — or the community? I've thought about that question a great deal. My answer to myself is that I don't think so. I did raise the issues. I did make those concerns my own. I did set out to educate the communities on these questions because I did not know how a person could be an educated Christian, a thinking Christian, a Christian without dealing with them. But I did not require any kind of allegiance to them. I do admit, however, that when I started a community newsletter I called it "The Leaven." Why? Because, though the word "justice" is used only one time in the Rule, it is, ironically, in the chapter on "What Kind of Person the Abbess Ought to Be." And the principle is plain. The chapter reads: "The Abbess ought not to teach or ordain or command anything which is against the Lord's precepts; on the contrary, her commands and her teaching should be a leaven of divine justice kneaded into the minds of the disciples." It's hard to be more direct than that.

No amount of medieval habits could have been a more ringing witness to the place of religious life in the public dialogue of a modern world.

27

Committed to the Wisdom of the Group

T HE CORPORATE COMMITMENT became more than merely a compass to community theory. It became a disposition whose direction was forward. It became a road whose name was justice. It became a journey whose name was lonely. And it became, at the same time, a destination. The destination, however, was what it had always been for Benedictines: a common search for God's will for the world, however difficult the discernment. Most of all, it was straight and unyielding. It marked every step of the community way.

There were internal skirmishes to be resolved at every juncture as the implications of the corporate commitment for the web of justice around the world became more and more focused: Should we put up "Nuclear Free Zone" signs on all our buildings? Should we use the little money we had to free our own natural gas reserves rather than be part of depending on the rest of the world for them? Should we begin to use universal language rather than male language only in our choral prayer? Should we stop using nonbiodegradable Styrofoam plates for community events? Should we close the community's girls' academy, more than a hundred years old, trusting that the corporate commitment was really our new identity?

With every resolution of every question, the power of the corporate commitment to effect both the direction and the impact of the group, and the individuals within it as well, became clearer and clearer.

In the best Benedictine tradition, every question became a community reflection. Every answer became a public witness. Every new situation began a new reprise of principles and practice.

There are two ways to effect change: by fiat or by consensus. One is immediate; the other can be painfully slow. I chose slow, not out of fear but out of a commitment to get wherever we were going together. Too many people had been left behind for too long in the early stages of renewal. We could not risk that again, or this time, I was certain, we would not survive it.

To change by fiat is fast and efficient and unpredictable. Many communities did just that. But then, when the person who had ordered the change left office renewal left office too. Communities slipped back or simply stopped and became frozen in a time warp that was neither here nor there. In some cases, the wounds of change went on festering for years. In others, change, though apparently official, never really penetrated the group.

To change by degrees, at the end of a long, hard process of group discussion, group negotiation, group consensus, group support, is slow, agonizingly slow, but stronger for that very reason. When the decision is finally made, it is a group decision. People own it and, sad as they may be about it, they will support it.

"Process," the substratum of consensual decision-making, is a natural by-product of an educated society. Communication theorists of the twentieth century began to study closely the newly emerging question of how to utilize the talents of an entire group, a problem that was basically new to a world fresh from monarchs and peasants, from the divine right of kings, hereditary authority, and global illiteracy. By the dawn of the twentieth century, for the first time in history, almost everyone could read and write, compulsory education had been introduced, and nations were being governed by civil servants and citizen patriots, whose offices and status disappeared with the turning of the calendar.

At the same time, corporations, governments, and systems were getting larger by the day. The labor movement had already exploded in the faces of the corporate kings who were still intent on treating the new breed of industrial workers in the style of the old wandering peasant class of earlier eras. Now systems everywhere were demanding basic civil rights and the chance to participate in making the rules that governed them. Vatican II itself had recognized the concepts of "collegiality" and "subsidiarity," the notion that decisions needed to arise out of the experience of the situation, rather than be imposed from some remote but supreme patriarch above them.

The world, and religious congregations with it, began to understand that "process" demanded a system to create, capture, discuss, and weigh all possible modes of actions. Process is not simply a series of questions designed to evoke yes or no answers so a group can get on with implementing the leader's ideas. Leaders who use process planning set out to discover all possible answers from all members of the group to any given question. It is not a quick quest for the immediate acceptable answer. It's not authoritarianism hiding behind a few ill-asked questions for the sake of getting ill-formed but affirming conclusions. It doesn't say "we talked about this" when what it means is that this was on the agenda once. It's saying, "What do you think we should do?" and really meaning it. Process planning is a synonym for trust.

Process planning doesn't rush decisions; it doesn't push decisions through; it doesn't put more emphasis on the decision than it does on the process itself. The purpose of process is to ensure the participation of every member of the group and to review together all the ideas that emerge, not simply the ones that may arise in one segment of a group only. It is an open hearing of all pros and cons, a group discussion and evaluation of all recommendations. Process takes time and demands the vision it takes to raise a group's questions early enough to give a group the space it needs to decide them.

Of all the operational decisions facing the community in 1978, the financial condition of St. Benedict Academy was the most serious and the potentially most impacting on the future of the group. Of all the decisions that were made, none tested our understanding of either consensual decision-making or the corporate commitment more.

There were myriad reasons to keep the academy open and great community commitment to do so: most members of the community had themselves graduated from there. It was the only public institution owned and operated by the community in Erie. Without the academy we would disappear from the face of the local map. It had the only special education program in the Catholic high school system in the city. Without St. Benedict Academy, what would happen to children in that program? It was the only inner-city Catholic high school in the area. It carried out the corporate commitment and its rejection of nuclearism to the hilt.

What's more, the faculty, past and present, was devoted to the place. Easy for the rest of us to write it off so easily, but not for them — a situation that meant internal ramifications for community life as well as a public shift of emphasis.

The only real reason to close the academy was a financial one in a community that was already bearing too heavy a debt for its size.

The conversation took ten full years. The advantages and disadvantages of every possible approach were opened for discussion. We could look for support grants, some suggested. We could have a special fundraising campaign. We could solicit money from alumnae. We could become coeducational. We could expand our offerings into junior high. We could build new facilities to attract more students.

Every idea was listed, examined, discussed. Every attempt was the subject of a review, report, and reexamination at every community meeting. Fund raising events and fee changes followed one after another. Most of all, the academy operated under financial strictures imposed by the community Chapter to control the debt. We could absorb a loss of $100,000 we decided, not a penny more. If the debt went beyond that figure, the decision to close would be automatic.

Could we have sold land to maintain the program? Could we have pressured sisters to go back to the academy staff in order to eliminate the problem of lay salaries? Probably. But did we want to barter our future to subsidize our past? Did we want to stamp out the new life that was going on in so many other facets of our ministry?

In the end, after years of discussion and discernment and mutual support, after years of trying to avoid the inevitable, we were all ready. The academy closed and opened again three months later as St. Benedict Education Center, which soon became one of the most effective welfare training schools for the unemployed and uncertified in the state of Pennsylvania. St. Benedict Academy lives, resurrected as a new kind of educational establishment that is as important now to the city, and the corporate commitment, as St. Benedict Academy ever was. The only difference is that now its population is just as needy as the German immigrants before it — but neither German nor Catholic.

Too fast a decision to close the academy could have scarred the community internally for years. Too slow a decision could have weighed down the community with additional debt to the point that it might never have survived. One by one we examined every idea together and together made a decision all of us could own. There were tears the day we made the final decision. I cried too. But I was crying as much about the sense of unity that came from making such a difficult decision together as I was at the thought of having to close such a wonderful piece of the past. I knew now that we truly could do anything we set out to do, that we had not dissolved as a community, that we were on our way to a new future together.

Trusting the wisdom of the group summoned the energies of the group and gave a whole new impetus to the age-old teaching ministry of the order.

In Erie, the way was not always simple, nor was it always easy to make new decisions, to let go of the past, to let happen the future, to take on a worldview rather than an institution as your identity. But it got clearer by the year. By the time the corporate commitment had been reviewed for the third time, it had been expanded to read: "To model the Benedictine charism of peace, Pax, by working for disarmament, ecological stewardship and social justice in solidarity with the poor and oppressed, especially women." The "signs of the times," John XXIII had said in the encyclical *Pacem in Terris* years before, "are nuclear weapons, poverty and the women's movement." Now the Erie Benedictines had themselves come to all three.

28

The Ongoing Struggle to Grow

P LEDGED NOW to stand with the poorest of the poor around the world, the community embarked on a series of activities that caused changes in lifestyle and the internal operations of the group as well as its public reputation.

When a migrant worker program in Erie asked to use the Mount in order to be nearer the grape arbors in which the migrants worked, the question seemed simple enough. There were empty classrooms in the basement, after all, which were once meant to be study rooms for large groups of young sisters and were now standing empty. Of course, the program would be welcome. But not really. Not yet. Not so fast. "Do you realize what those people could bring into this house?" one sister asked. "At least you'll have to put up a metal gate to keep them in one hall."

The thought of "laypeople" — "that kind of people" — in our own living space was a step beyond what years of separation from the laity had prepared us to absorb. So the gate went up until security ceased to be an issue for us.

But even though the gate was forgotten as the months went by, there were still uncomfortable moments when young Hispanic women and their children spilled things on the dining room rug. Or got juice from the vending machine. Or interrupted the cafeteria line. It takes a lot of living to learn to live like human beings once you have become a world unto yourself. And we had to learn that.

Then global outreach became the goal. First I took the entire council to Cuernavaca for a study tour of Mexico, one of the poorest countries of the world, which sat on the border of the richest. How could we possibly make decisions in our own lives, as a community, unless we understood that their lives depended so much on us as Americans?

The week was a long one for women whose lives had been spent in offices and classrooms. Water came through the roof above our beds at night. The toilets were seldom flushed. Day tours to Indian villages at the top of the mountains or to the squatters' huts along the railroad tracks across the gorge plagued us. Catechists from Latin American countries testified to the torture of catechists by young soldiers trained in the art by U.S. "consultants." The catechists were teaching peasants that Jesus wanted liberation for the poor, and that, the politicians decided, hinted at sedition. The Vatican documents called religious life "the prophetic dimension of the church." What were we doing as a council, as a community, to witness to these injustices?

Frustration became the order of the day. We were trying to function on the local level and link the local level to the global level at the same time. Our vision was broader now, but the days weren't any longer and the daily demands weren't any less than they had ever been. What's more, we were a Benedictine community with its ongoing daily round of choral prayer periods and the fullness of community life with all that implied on the human level — celebrations, deaths, hospitality, personal problems, as well as a sister's professional obligations. But as Moses sent out scouts in the desert to determine what was ahead of us, so did we.

Sisters began to move freely into Third World programs and conferences and projects, always coming back wiser, always coming back stronger for having done it, always coming back more committed to the notion of a corporate commitment than ever. They went to the Yucatan and Haiti and Nicaragua and Ethiopia and the Soviet Union. Like emissaries from the heart of the empire, we went out to see for ourselves what life was like for most of the rest of the world so we could live more intensely Christian lives at home.

At the same time, parents and pastors felt abandoned and called the community "unfaithful to their vows" — as did sisters themselves who saw the communities in which they had lived for years become smaller and smaller as sisters moved on to other works.

But, at the same time, though we were leaving the schools, we went deeper and deeper into the inner city all the while we were going further out into the world. When the phone call came asking if the Erie Benedictines would take over the management of the Erie Community Food Bank, newly developed and barely surviving, I put down the phone knowing we didn't have the resources to do it and knowing at the same time that we had to do it anyway. And we did. Food distribution to the poor went from 440,000 pounds of food per year in 1982 to 5.5 million pounds in 1992. The soup kitchen expanded till it became the largest food provider in the diocese. The food pantry opened to serve the poor elderly, the working poor, and the unemployed.

Americans obviously had to learn to shepherd our own resources rather than take for granted that we could forever go on sucking the life out of others. So the community drilled a gas well with money we had from the sale of a stock once gifted to the community and then forgotten. We had received the stock at $50,000 years before and, when I realized that it was still on the community books, I ordered it sold. "We're not a brokerage firm," I argued. "We should get rid of it."

At just that moment a drilling company in the area wanted to lease land from us in order to drill wells for investors. I would have allowed it. After all, why let the land just sit there if its resources could be released into the public trust? And the community agreed. Nevertheless, a full one-third of the community, in which a high degree of consensus had become the norm, disapproved. "If we had the money to drill a well," they argued on the chapter floor, "we should drill it ourselves, not encourage more commercial profiteering."

Concerned about that high a degree of reluctance in a community that had long ago chosen trust over contention, I refused to complete the lease. That afternoon, the finance officer told me in a completely unrelated discussion that "the old stock finally sold today." "For how much?" I wanted to know. "For $110,000," she told me. I thought for a moment. "How much did they say it would cost to drill a well?" I asked. The treasurer consulted her notes. "$110,000." The handwriting on the wall seemed pretty clear to me. The well produced for over thirty years, signaling that there was an abundance of natural gas in the area if others wanted to drill for it. At the same time it released additional community monies for other projects.

In an age when the world was in dire need of renewable energy sources, we put up the highest windmill in the country in order to test the viability of wind energy off Lake Erie. We put in solar panels to heat the swimming pool at camp and the greenhouse at the monastery although scientific articles on the subject said that Erie was not suitable for solar energy. It was a roll of the dice that won on all counts. It was the kind of risk that would not profit us as much as the information that was gained could profit others. It was the kind of thing Cistercians had done in France in the thirteenth century when they refused all gifts of land but the worst of them so they could teach others how to farm them.

We brought in speakers from around the world and from multiple religions: rabbis, Buddhist monks, Protestant theologians and philosophers, scientists and activists. They stretched the horizons of our own souls. The national borders of the world were blurring into one another everywhere. There were issues in conflict everywhere. We had to begin to understand how God was working in other people. We had to make ourselves — and the monastery — a bridge over differences. But first, we had to puncture the religious ghettoes in our own minds in which we had all grown up.

To do that, the education of the community had to be ongoing, regular, and in common. It was no longer enough simply

to educate individual sisters to points of high-level special-
ization. In order to maintain a universe of discourse among
ourselves that was broad enough, deep enough to prepare the
community to change in a changing world, it had to be continual. And it had to be open to other experiences, other insights,
other ways of seeing God. Change could not be allowed to
surprise us again.

We put up a world flag on the flagpole beside the front door
instead of the American flag. Later we flew the world flag above
the American flag to show both a global and U.S. identity. The
very sight of this sent people flying to their congressperson
to complain about us; they in turn threatened our tax status.
And sisters had trouble with it too. "My brother was a prisoner
of war in World War II," one said. "I feel that this is some
kind of treason." We compromised: the world flag would fly on
Mondays, Wednesdays, and Fridays; the American flag would
fly on Tuesdays, Thursdays, and Saturdays. On Sundays, the
Lord's Day, no flag would fly at all. It wasn't long before all the
partisans forgot why they had been so committed to any flag
and every day became the Lord's Day, with no flag at all.

We went on in the same ways and with the same kind of
people we had always served in inner-city Erie — the people
on the lower end of the social class, those who had come late
to this country or this area or this system — but we began to
serve them differently. We had operated a girl's academy for
college-bound students or businesswomen for over a hundred
years. Now we turned our attention to providing job training
and placement programs for unemployed adults.

We opened retreat and spirituality programs for women. We
expanded the liturgical arts to make the Eucharist an experience of the gospel rather than simply an exercise of the faith.
We created a team of chaplains rather than continue the practice of having a resident chaplain whose style, over the years,
could come to cramp our own liturgical needs.

With donor dollars we built hermitages in the woods behind
the monastery to provide a fuller experience of Benedictine life
for guests: deep reflection, love of silence, and renewed energy

for the striving soul. To this day, the hermitages have never been empty.

Finally, having learned to think for ourselves as women, to see our own oppression, our own invisibility, even in the church, we began to lobby for women's rights everywhere. We edited hymns and office books to begin to pray this time not just in English but in universal English so that God could be seen in all God's glory, not simply as an icon of maleness. We began to include women in every dimension of prayer and sacrament. We began to preach our own sermons. We began to voice the spirituality we were living. We began to grow in self-confidence as thinkers, as artists, as voices of the gospel.

We began to live inside a new theological world. We set out to be what we hoped the world would become: just, free, equal, and fully adult. And, in the course of it, we became a haven for women and men who were looking for both a political and an ecclesiastical world that was more a circle than a pyramid.

I remember very well the Sunday morning I went into a chapel packed with people I did not know. Ironically, it happened the weekend I had decided to resign as prioress so the community could elect someone whose positions were less well known and would therefore be less a liability than I was. After all, as the corporate commitment got clearer and clearer, donations had dropped. Benefactors had disappeared. The old friends of the monastery had drifted away. Thinking I must have missed notice of some kind of public event being held in our chapel, I said to the sister at the door, "Who are these people?" She raised her eyebrows and kept passing out the eucharistic worship aids for the day. "I don't have a clue," she said.

After Mass that morning, I deliberately left chapel first in order to meet people coming out of chapel. Most of them were young couples. Some of them had driven for miles to attend Mass at the Mount. "What brought you all this way?" I asked one after the other. "We heard about you," one young man said. "We want to be part of a community that thinks like this about these things." The chapel was never empty again.

I didn't resign. After all, Vatican II was still in the making, and I didn't want to miss it.

It was a totally new experience of both church and state, of being female instead of neutered observers of the world around us, of being agents of the faith rather than simply consumers of the faith.

The answer to "What did we grow up for?" was beginning to come into focus. We grew up for the sake of the world. "I know well the plans I have in mind for you," God says through Jeremiah in scripture, "plans for your welfare not for woe." We knew now that we were meant to be part of bringing God's plan, God's wellness to the world, rather than simply bearing up under the woe.

Now the full criteria for renewal had been addressed.

In one era, we had concentrated on reclaiming the charism of Benedictinism by giving ourselves over to searching for the will of God in the Word of God.

In another era, we concentrated on giving ourselves over to the building of human community both in us and around us.

In a third stage, we rediscovered the role of religious life by giving over our resources to minister to a wounded world.

For some of us, it had been the work of a lifetime. For others, it had been a struggle between two lifetimes. For the rest of us, for newer members of the community, it was an investment in the future, not for ourselves and our own salvation this time, but for the sake of the world whose welfare we held in our own hands.

At the same time, a very old community life was becoming new again.

29

Still Full of Sap,
Still Green

S O WHAT HAPPENED to religious life between 1960 and
1990? Hindsight makes clear what we didn't realize when
we began: we started out focused on theological renewal
and found ourselves totally consumed by the questions of
organizational revitalization that theological renewal implied.

What we know now we know surely: revitalization is not a
haphazard event. It is not something that simply happens to a
group, out of the blue, unplanned, surprisingly. Revitalization
is the conscious process of being willing to live newly in a new
and changing world even when others are not new and the
world does not yet want change.

Revitalization begs for commitment to the long haul. The
revitalization process brings with it learnings about life, about
authority, about vision, about responsibility that cannot be
gleaned in eras of development when riding the crest of new
beginnings seems as if it will never end.

Revitalization teaches chiefly that change does not happen
overnight, that change is a dark night in a cold desert, that
it can take a hundred years before the world knows if social
change has really happened or not. People with a need for
instantaneous satisfaction need not apply.

Revitalization has certain clear characteristics. It is nurtured
by some things, discouraged by others.

The transformation of an institution is as much an emotional enterprise as it is an intellectual one. Just because buggy

whip makers know that cars have been invented does not mean that they will automatically begin to reshape their own businesses to make tires or alternators.

Just because a religious community finally begins to realize that candidates to religious life will no longer be seventeen years old does not mean that they will begin to focus their attention on the spiritual gifts and needs of older women. In fact, adjusting to older candidates has been a major problem for some religious communities for the last twenty years. They may know that their youngest members are in their forties but go on dealing with them as if they were seventeen.

Just because religious congregations face the fact that the "war vocations" — the large number of aspirants to religious life generated by the increased attention to spiritual issues during a time of social crisis — will no longer be the norm does not mean that they will be able to envision a role for smaller, more dynamic groups whose purpose is to animate society rather than to staff institutions.

Institutions that are open to revitalization — meaning not neurotic — operate on open lines of communication. Before Vatican II, Benedictines went to meetings just as regularly as they do now. But they didn't go there to discuss their lives together or to make community decisions together. They went to hear what the superior said they should do. Then they "voted" for it.

In the healthy group, a group that is strong enough to change in order to remain as effective as they have always been, small groups of select people do not make all the decisions. Participation, process, group brainstorming, the exploration of various rationales and differences of opinion are valued highly and encouraged regularly. "Discussion" is not a euphemism for being given the right to ask questions about plans that have already been made.

In a healthy group, ideas begin in one of two places — from the group and from the leadership — not simply from the leadership. There is no breakdown in communication, no

organizational dysfunction in the name of authority, no institutional depression. The healthy group thrives on information
and seeks it from everywhere.

For a group to achieve revitalization, the group must share a
common set of values, norms, and ideals that have been commonly defined. A group that is divided about its essence or its
direction can never get to a new place together with the kind
of vigor it will take to sustain it there.

The healthy group shares a high sense of meaning and significance. It does not doubt its ability to succeed at whatever it
chooses to undertake together. When it becomes apparent that
some activities have served their purpose, having to go on to
new things does not reduce it to despair.

The healthy group is in touch with the reality in which it
lives. It does not alienate itself from society. It does not cut
itself off in the name of otherwordliness or sanctity, as religious
communities had been made to do, from what it means to
be a spiritual human being in this time and this place. The
healthy group is not divided, not afraid, not confused about
its purpose, not unclear about its priorities. At its worst in the
renewal process, the small community in Erie had been all of
that — polarized, rigid, hostile, and paralyzed. Renewal did not
happen in Erie until the group as group chose to move beyond
its institutional neuroses, either because they believed in what
was happening or because they decided to embrace the process
and see what happened. They simply determined to trust one
another again.

The fact is that change is blocked by frozen leadership, by
authoritarianism, by paralyzing interpersonal conflicts, and by
a general fear of making a paradigm shift, of being willing to
see their world differently. When, immersed in a process they
trusted, the group began to feel in control of their lives again,
the fear fell away.

For religious communities, the paradigm shift was a theological shift lost in a social shift. Our world had been totally
upended by science and the assaults of social science on false
assumptions about gender, hierarchy, and individualism.

The revitalized organization is action-centered. It defines what it intends to do and does it. Then it transmits the message over and over again, in every way possible: "We are not a failure. We are changing, not running away, not being unfaithful to the mission, not dying." Just changing. Just becoming what we are in new ways for a new time. Just becoming what we've always been — but newly.

We began to communicate with our friends and families, then even with strangers at every possible community event, through magazines and newspapers, through books and speeches. We taught Benedictinism and how we were now living it in every way we knew how.

We concentrated on economic viability, refusing to subsidize works we'd done for years simply because we'd always done them when the needs did not justify the efforts.

We stopped providing services when people stopped asking for those services anymore in the numbers we had been accustomed to expecting. Instead we began to concentrate on new endeavors that would allow us to serve new people in new ways. We never closed one thing without announcing the opening of another in its place. We were not about death and diminishment of yesterday's successes; we were about now. We closed the academy and immediately opened the new Educational Center. We closed the Hospitality House at Pax Center and immediately opened Pax Christi, USA, in Erie, under the auspices of the Erie Benedictines until that group could become stabilized under lay leadership. We continued a summer youth camp but expanded the programming to include adult groups and retreat work. We reduced the size of the music department and began a bell choir for liturgical expression instead. We left the grade schools and opened housing for low-income and handicapped elderly.

Clearly, innovation is the chief characteristic of an energized and energizing group. Not more of the same for its own sake. Not just the same-old, same-old. "How did you get so many new things started here?" people asked in amazement when they looked at the number of community ministries, the amount of community involvement, the personal energy of the group. In an age when conventional wisdom said that religious life was dying, they saw one thing after another being opened. They saw the gift shop, the artists, the musicians, the publishing efforts, the gardeners, the inner-city ministries, the absorption of lay guests, the youth programs, the ecological projects, the spirituality centers, the public administrators and consultants, the mission work, the hospitality work, the public education programs, the peace and justice work. "How could you possibly do all this at a time like this?" they wondered in amazement. "I didn't," I said. "All I did was listen to what each of the sisters said she wanted to do," I went on. "If you come back in ten years, we do not promise you that any of these particular activities will still exist. I do hope that we can promise you that we will still be following the gifts of our members."

The revitalized group never stops "experimenting." They do not exist to do tomorrow only what they did yesterday. They simply keep improving it, stretching it, making it new again.

Most of all, they intend to succeed. They intend to become new over and over again. They are here to serve now, not yesterday. They are monastic communities, not monastic museums.

We invited the city into the monastery. We began an associate program by which "associate members" could join the community for ministry, prayer, and personal development. They became part of us and we became a stronger monastery for doing it. At that time there were thirty Oblates; now that the two groups have merged there are over two hundred.

And will it last? What will the future hold?

It all depends on whether we go on participating and innovating as well as praying and working. Given leaders with vision enough to ask questions and then to listen to the community's answers, given a community with a clear sense of mission, given a group that is infused with a sense of basic Benedictine values and purpose, and an internal climate that creates the processes and conditions for innovation, experimentation, genuine discussion, and creativity, the future is secure.

But that takes a great spiritual depth. It means that translating basic Benedictine values of community, stewardship, peace, individual needs, hospitality, flexibility, moderation, and the spiritual life must always mean more to the group — more to the leadership — than structures, rules, bureaucratic authority, and custom.

It may even mean that Alice's witness to freedom of spirit, Mary Margaret's sense of love and openness, and what I learned from the two of them about the place of social justice and the centrality of creativity in a Benedictine community must go on.

Benedictine life does not exist for itself alone. In that awareness lies the real challenge of conversion. Benedictine life does not immerse a person in complacency and spiritual consolations. It requires spiritual discipline for the sake of spiritual growth, the real essence of its conversion. It exists to model the reign of God that must someday, surely, come.

Now that we have grown up, now that conversion of heart demanded in this new century has finally been faced, has finally been begun, we must never again stop asking what we grew up for. If we do that, no one ever again will wonder. We won't be there to ask.

Epilogue

T HE TWENTIETH CENTURY ranks in history as a crossover moment in time. One world — the agricultural, nationalistic, parochial, and isolated one — was giving way to a new one marked by instant communications, global technology, pluralistic societies, and seeping boundaries — but we didn't see it then. We grew up thinking that life would always be what we thought it was then. We expected the country to be white, our political, social, and economic worlds to be constant, and the church to be unchanging. Especially the church. But it wasn't. In fact, none of them were.

Instead we found all of them in flux and our own attitudes and ideas about all of them in flux as well. It worried us, irritated us, put us into political and ecclesial camps we never before even knew existed. Slowly, in the midst of the impasse, religious began to realize that if we were ever to be able to move forward together again, we all needed two things: some change in direction, yes, but some change of heart about it too. We needed a broader vision, an understanding of change, an experience of conversion.

Change and conversion, we finally came to realize, are not the same thing.

The question is, what, if anything, does all this exploration of the ending of one era of religious life and the beginning of another mean — to religious life in particular, to groups in general, to the church as a whole? What can an inside look at the struggles of one particular religious community, once considered frozen in time, more otherworldly than real, mean to the rest of humankind? Well, for those who lived through it, it means both the obvious and the not-so-obvious.

The obvious implication stuns us with the power of its simplicity. Life is not static. None of us, no matter how much we would like to, no matter how deeply we think we should, can stop the reeling of the globe. We cannot not change.

Change is required of us all. No one and nothing can stand still, cemented in the place, the work, the era that we had come to take for granted. However comforting the thought, however desirable the situation, what I am now, where I am now, will not always be.

We change internally as we age. The world around us changes externally as its sciences, populations, and social systems expand. Even the personal situations and relationships and roles in which we exist change without our bidding. What we learned to expect in life does not happen. What we cling to disappears. The institutions on which we have built our entire identity fade and die, no longer the energy center of the universe in which I live. Being a railroad conductor ceases to be important in an age of air travel, for instance. Or I'm not reelected to the position that was once the center of my whole life. Or the parishes close, or merge, or become empty memories of what once was. Or, more basic than any of these, what I learned about God and sin and grace and goodness come to new bloom without my bidding.

Those things give frame to the obvious: change is a constant on all levels, in all the dimensions of life. That cannot be ignored. It can only be accepted and so must be coped with if we are to weather the stages of life, of institution, of relationships through which every life must pass.

Change will happen. Our only decision is whether to engage it or resist it. If we engage change, we can shape it. If we resist it, we run the risk of being shriveled by it into less than we are meant to be.

No, all change is not good, not permanent, not life-giving. Some of it is fad. Some of it is destructive. But all change is change. It cannot be ignored. It cannot be denied. It must be integrated into life and its moorings.

The not-so-obvious dimension of life is even more demanding than the obvious constancy of change, however. The not-so-obvious part of change is that change alone does not define the measure of our growth. Only conversion can do that. Only the willingness to embrace change, to learn from it, and to recognize in it the stuff of my own ultimate development can possibly give change its coinage.

If an excursion through the changes set off by the tremors of Vatican II have anything to say to the rest of the world it is surely that conversion is the only virtue that can possibly save, faithfully negotiate the modern age. Otherwise, the world will find itself immersed in wars of reaction that cannot possibly prevail in a changing world or they will be fruitlessly engaged in wars of reform that cannot possibly win the hearts of a people, no matter how successfully they seem to have controlled their behaviors. The Taliban who wanted to go back to Islamic fundamentalism in Afghanistan proved one part of the equation, the shah of Iran who wanted to Westernize the country by fiat proved the other.

Instead, conversion requires that we hold to the essence of the faith, up close and unadorned, while it takes new shape around us.

Conversion requires the humility to look again at what we always knew to be true and see new truth in it.

Conversion requires the willingness to risk. The miracle of the Red Sea, the Talmud says, is not that the waters parted. The miracle of the Red Sea is that the first Jew walked through it. Stepping out into a new universe of grace and gift is the challenge of conversion. It is the ability to admit that there may be more to life than my own small perspective on it.

Finally, conversion requires leadership that is also capable of learning, of trust, of questions, of faith. In the end, if the history of this one group of women religious teaches us anything at the outset of an age in which change is more rapid than at any other time of history, it will be the kind of leadership we foster that is key to the process.

Leadership counts. But leadership and authoritarianism are not the same thing. Authoritarianism, devoid of ideas, simply uses a group for the flush of controlling it. "My throne," "my country," "my community," "my parish," "my diocese" are all dimensions of the same kind of patriarchal system that invests all knowledge and all control in the hands of the person at the top of the pyramid. Everyone else in systems such as this, in the end, simply serve to carry out the will of the sovereign.

Authoritarianism is nothing more than raw power seeking personal sovereignty.

Leadership, on the other hand, does not "control" a group. Leadership reads the culture in which the group exists and then provides the resources the group will need to respond to the demands the culture makes of the group. Leadership does not answer questions; it simply raises them early enough to enable a group to find its own answer before the needs of the culture outstrip the gifts of the group.

Where there is real leadership there is more concentration on vision than on rules. Leadership does not trouble itself with the operational, the mundane, the regulatory. Visionary leaders allow the people on-site to handle the demands of the daily. They concentrate on what is coming, not on the details of things at hand.

A wise old bishop for whom the Erie Benedictines once taught, for instance, asked every new sister sent to teach in the parish schools of which he was pastor what she would do if the fire alarm sounded. If, he warned us, she didn't say, "Call the fire department," rather than, "Report it to the superior," he would send her back to the motherhouse in Erie. There was a time, his answer implied, whatever distorted notions of the vow of obedience might insinuate to the contrary, when religious needed to be able to act on their own.

Authoritarianism, the traditional mode of religious leadership, the story pointed out, clearly had limitations, even at the height of its theological development. Authoritarianism and leadership, the bishop knew, were not synonyms.

Leadership does not immerse itself in the details of the immediate; administrators do that. Leadership requires prescience, an appreciation for the challenges of the future. The function of leadership is not to maintain the past or keep up with the present. It is to inculcate a healthy regard for the future, to enable a group to change so that it can, in essence, go on remaining the same. It is meant to prepare a group to deal with challenges to come, not simply to oversee the tasks of the present. It is a rare and sacred trust. Not everyone can do it. In fact, not everyone wants to do it. The signs of authoritarianism, often benign but always closed, are clear: "because I said so" or "I am the prioress and this is my decision" become the order of the day, sometimes silently, always clearly. But when authority postures itself as divinity in action, the will of God, the work of the Holy Spirit in the other members of the community is smothered.

A good many religious communities, for instance, did not complete the renewal cycle because the internal tensions inherent in institutional renewal became the fodder of division rather than energy for new life. Superiors formed in the authoritarian model fought to keep control of the process of renewal, to define limits, to themselves determine what would be the group's new directions, and to put boundaries around the creativity of the group. They wanted to "renew" the group — but they wanted to do it without changing themselves.

Meant to lead, they chose instead to direct the process themselves, just as the authoritarian models from a more static past had done, rather than release the group, trust the group, lead the group to find for themselves the answers to what it meant to be religious now and here and in the modern world.

Eventually, exhausted by the pushing and pulling of authoritarian processes, without the benefit of having been led to discover their own newly internalized direction, too many groups did not survive. When religious needed to be able to mobilize all the energy they had simply to adjust to new ideas and conditions, they found themselves pitted against the sacralization of the past in the very persons of those who were supposed to be leading them to renew it. Having sacralized the beginnings of the group, they forgot, if they ever knew, the kind of creative tumult out of which it had come.

Leaders, on the other hand, enable groups to grow by opening questions rather than stifling them, by enabling change rather than resisting it, by tolerating the kind of chaos it takes to create — and re-create — a group.

At the same time, no amount of leadership, however creative, can save the group that refuses to accept it. Groups can simply refuse to pursue the questions before them. They can become sects in the heart of the community.

Groups can hide from the present. They can deny that the present situation really demands anything different from the past, not change, not conversion of heart. They can blame the leader for misleading them. They can confuse cosmetic change with the kind of new commitment that is necessary to turn to new goals with the same driving force with which they once pursued the tasks of the past.

Whatever the motives, in the end the facts speak for themselves: authoritarian or not, no institution really functions by fiat at all. Scholars have noted for years, in fact, that the person at the top of any organization is in a very vulnerable position.[15]

Whether an order has authority is determined by the person to whom it is addressed, not by the person who gives it. To say that we are not permitted to do something simply means that we ourselves, for some other reason, have decided not to become agents of our own lives. Whether an order is obeyed, for instance, depends simply upon whether there is enough power to back it up and hold it there forever. For what we consider to be our own survival we may decide to accept an order that blocks our own growth or conscience or needs.

But history is clear, nevertheless: eventually, the deep-down will of a society always breaks through the cement of old traditions to new life. The church did eventually reform, for instance, whatever the stringent, even murderous, attempts to stop the reformers. Democracy did eventually supersede monarchies. A money society did eventually wear away the barter system — though every one of these major cultural changes was called sin or ruination at its inception by someone who had the power to try to stop the changes.

A good many czars and popes and potentates have discovered to their peril the truth of their dependence on the will of the populace for their success. When the members of a group withhold cooperation, it simply dissolves the authority of the authority. Members, in fact, have a great deal of power, more than is commonly realized, to determine the direction of an organization.

Perhaps in no place in recent history has the assailability of the leader been more apparent than it was during the period of the renewal of religious communities. Groups blissfully unaware of the rising tide of change around them went on for years without attempting to update either internal practices or external works. Canon laws had made evolutionary change impossible. Questions were unacceptable. Superiors attended most of all to "maintaining the religious spirit" of the houses — read: to maintaining adherence to the rules and regulations of the past. But then came Vatican II and its mandate that religious communities update their lifestyle according to "the charism of the founder, the needs of the members, and the signs of the times." Then, groups and leaders discovered the power of the group.

After the call of Vatican II for the renewal of religious congregations, good leaders negotiated the pitch and rolls of change, sparked by the needs of the members themselves. But in too many places "the last error seemed worse than the first." The rising pressure for changes long overdue split many communities, destroyed some, moved others in completely new directions. Suddenly women who had been "gaggled" everywhere they went for most of their lives either began to resist being driven, began to move outside the school of nuns who had moved to and fro together all their lives, or, conversely, found themselves uncertain about what to do without the herding tactics of a lifetime. Then change ceased to be a theoretical construct about social development and took on a life of its own, deep in the souls, down in the center of the psyches of sisters who had been either too long suppressed to know they had been suppressed or too long herded to wait a minute longer for the system of suppression to be dismantled incrementally.

Religious congregations came alive with differences long undetected, always restrained. The organization began to stretch and breathe and groan and crack the carapace of changelessness. Then the genie was out of the bottle.

An organization is a system of movable parts that moves at its own pace, in its own way, for its own purposes. It is a living organism as much subject to all the vagaries of time and change as any other living thing around it. The only difference is that until Vatican II, religious didn't know it. We thought that religious life as we lived it then was immutable, cast in stone, revealed for all time and places. We were wrong.

Religious life did not die as a result of renewal, did not evaporate, did not abandon its compass points. It simply became more of what it was meant to be: a way of life in search of the God of the Daily, whatever the situation, whenever the era, whatever the shape of the system in which they now found themselves. They knew now that it was what they were about that mattered, not that what they were about could never change.

After 125 years of one kind of service, they had, in the 25 years that followed it, learned a life lesson worth sharing: We are all here to live a gospel life. We are not here to perpetuate the institutions that from one age to another become its vehicle.

Change, conversion, and leadership, they knew now, are the anchors, the essence, of renewal. What group in the church has grappled with real renewal and not discovered the place of all three in the process. Where one or the other is lacking, renewal simply does not happen.

There may be, then, a great deal that one religious community — a way of life, a microcosm of church and society — has to say to the rest of humankind about what it means to change, to grow, to become what we are meant to be but become it differently than we had planned.

Notes

1. Stephanie Campbell, *Visions of Change, Voices of Challenge: The History of Renewal in the Benedictine Sisters of Erie 1958–1990* (Xlibris, 2001).

2. "Hannah Arendt," in the *New Yorker*, cited at www.ariga.com/frosties/hannaharendt.shtml.

3. Robert Nisbet, ed., *Social Change* (New York: Harper & Row, 1972), 1.

4. Decree on the Ministry and Life of Priests, no. 9.

5. Elting E. Morison, "Innovation: A Case Study," in *Social Change*, ed. Robert Nisbet (New York: Harper & Row, 1972), 124.

6. R. Freeman Butts, *The American Tradition in Religion and Education* (Boston: Beacon Press, 1950), 197–98.

7. Karl E. Weick, *The Social Psychology of Organizing* (Reading, Mass.: Addison-Wesley, 1969), 8.

8. Joan Chittister et al., *Climb along the Cutting Edge: An Analysis of Change in Religious Life* (New York: Paulist Press, 1977).

9. Charles A. Kiesler and Sara B. Kiesler, *Conformity* (Reading, Mass.: Addison-Wesley, 1969), 25, quoting Floyd Allport.

10. Ibid., 27.

11. Muzafer Sherif, *The Psychology of Social Norms* (New York: Harper & Row, 1966), 69, quoting F. H. Allport.

12. Kiesler and Kiesler, *Conformity*, 2.

13. Uri Merry and George I. Brown, *The Neurotic Behavior of Organizations* (Cleveland: Gestalt Institute of Cleveland Press, 1987).

14. Joan Chittister, "Ministry and Secularism," *New Catholic World* (March–April 1980): 74–79.

15. Weick, *The Social Psychology of Organizing*, 5.

Also by Joan Chittister

Illuminated Life
Monastic Wisdom for Seekers of Light
ISBN 1-57075-233-8

From Abandonment to Zeal, this alphabet of
monastic values helps us experience peace and love
in the midst of life's pressures and problems.

There Is a Season
With Art by John August Swanson
ISBN 1-57075-022-X

CATHOLIC BOOK AWARD, FIRST PLACE

"For everything there is a season . . ."
A glorious meditation in art and words on the famous
text from Ecclesiastes. Text and art together tell us:
The season is now. The time is ours. Live!

A Passion for Life
Fragments of the Face of God
With Icons by Robert Lentz
ISBN 1-57075-318-0

FIRST PLACE, CATHOLIC BOOK AWARD WINNER

"Offers the sort of soul-nourishing meditation found
only in the encounter with beauty." *–U.S. Catholic*

Please support your local bookstore, or call 1-800-258-5838.
For a free catalogue, please write us at
**Orbis Books, Box 308
Maryknoll NY 10545-0308**
or visit our website at www.orbisbooks.com

Thank you for reading *The Way We Were*.
We hope you enjoyed it.